FROM NORTHERN KENT

Edited by Simon Harwin

First published in Great Britain in 2000 by
YOUNG WRITERS
Remus House,
Coltsfoot Drive,
Woodston,
Peterborough, PE2 9JX
Telephone (01733) 890066

All Rights Reserved

Copyright Contributors 1999

HB ISBN 0 75431 850 8
SB ISBN 0 75431 851 6

FOREWORD

This year, the Young Writers' Future Voices competition proudly presents a showcase of the best poetic talent from over 42,000 up-and-coming writers nationwide.

Successful in continuing our aim of promoting writing and creativity in children, our regional anthologies give a vivid insight into the thoughts, emotions and experiences of today's younger generation, displaying their inventive writing in its originality.

The thought, effort, imagination and hard work put into each poem impressed us all and again the task of editing proved challenging due to the quality of entries received, but was nevertheless enjoyable. We hope you are as pleased as we are with the final selection and that you continue to enjoy *Future Voices From Northern Kent* for many years to come.

Contents

Tom Luck   1

Borden Grammar School

J Brincat	1
Stephen Wood	2
Shawn Tyrrell	2
Ben Wright	3
Matthew Horder	4
Jamie White	4
Gregory Brissenden	5
James Palmer	6
Christopher Dean	6
Liam Scarfe	7
Adam Mullins	7
Martin Spokes	8
Sean Parker	9
Aden Philpott	10
Peter Harris	10
A J Manning	11
Jason Mathew Willmore	12
Garry Walmsley	12
Scott Teague	13
Nick Brena	14
Lewis Peter Smith	14
Andrew Owens	15
Shane Dowle	16
Darren Nokes	16
Matthew Murdoch	17
Terry Seager	18
David Taylor	18
Christopher Payne	19
Matthew Mawson	20
Anthony Sage	20
Richard Barling	21
Phil Simpson	22
William Lay	23

Matthew Wood	24
Robert Wisniewski	24
Giles Gabriel	25
Stuart Green	26
Charles Ayre	27
Weiran Zhang	28
James Ashford	28
Marcus Patrick Newing	29
Carl O'Neill	30
William Tyrrell	31
Andrew Dickson	32
Kris Forshaw	32
Glen Johnson	33
Ashley Thomas	34
James Gibson	34
Adam Grigsby	35
Michael Evans	36
Neil Goodhew	36
Nathaniel Daniels	37
Vishal Mistry	38
Daniel Howard	38
Jacob Brown	39
James Loose	40
Christopher Beck	40
Luke Auron-Cotton	41
Darren Brown	42
Russell Cope	42
Paul Gregory	43
Chris Mills	43
Adam Britton-Mosley	44
Neil James Haffenden	45
James Stickens	45
Simon Meeks	46
Chris Bassett	46
Samuel Luckhurst	47
Tom Ralph	48
Ben Calder	49
Philip Hawkins	50

Clarendon House School
- Holly Horton — 51
- Harri Stenning — 51
- Jessica Turnbull — 51
- Emily Bath — 52
- Marie Brown — 52
- Tasmin Field — 53
- Beverley Watling — 53
- Sarah Doyle — 53
- Gemma Young — 54
- Jo Johnson — 54
- Leah O'Connor — 55
- Jenny Brown — 55
- Kirsty Barber — 56
- Abigail Ballard — 57
- Christina Michael — 57
- Victoria Moss — 58

Cranbrook School
- Robert Dickens — 59
- Kirsten Morris — 60
- Thomas Malcolm — 61
- Gemma Reyte — 62
- Louise Kirby — 63
- Camilla Hall — 64
- Lee Whalen — 64
- Stephanie Whitelaw — 65
- Rosie Donaldson — 66
- Francis Daly — 67
- Ed Vaughan — 68

Darrick Wood School
- Olivia Nation — 68
- Daniel Ordidge — 69
- Luke Frizoni — 69
- Adam Potter — 70
- Christine Wayne — 70
- Francesca Prudente — 71

Rimona Barabhuiya	72
Nicholas Foster	72
Stephen Tait	73
Lucy Hone	73
Natalie Bell	74
Natalie Pennington	74
Lucy Webb	75
Adam Law	76
Elizabeth Pennington	77
Carly Maunsell	77
Cheralyn Humphrey	78
Roxanna Garnett	78
Laurence Webb	79
Lauren Brown	80
Ashley Pope	80
Katherine Marshall	81
Laura Stewart	82
Samantha-Marie Harrington	82
Ryan Nicholls	83
Lauren Brett	84
Natalie Gardiner	85
Lizzie Ward	85
Scott Humphreys	86
Ruth Jones	86
Matthew Adams	87
Ben Turner	87
Daniel Hoath	88
William Marsh	89
Claire Lincoln	89

Dartford Grammar School For Girls

Sonia Chana	90
Nafisa Baba-Ahmed	91

Gravesend Grammar School For Girls

Kirsten King	92
Holly McLean	92
Oneet Sandher	93

Charlotte Irving	94
Lucy Fowler	95
Emma Townsend	96
Suzannah Flynn	96
Katie Smith	97
Paula Smith	97
Louise Aldous	98
Rebecca Drewry	99
Michelle Smith	100
Julia Marshall	101
Caroline Savin	102
Keely Underdown	103
Skye Fenton	104
Kayleigh Gilchrist	105
Sophie Cable	106
Hannah Bishop	107
Katie Greenwood	108
Aimee Long	109
Sarah Payne	110
Rachel Willett	111
Sally Russell	112
Emma Drummond	113
Johanna Nixon	114
Jennifer O'Brien	115
Sophie Muckart	116
Jessica Dossena	117

Hartsdown Technology College

James Quinn	117
Vikki Spain-Gower	118
Jake Tait	118
Philip Shepherd	119
Danielle Moon	119
Neal Sullivan	120
Lydia Cassar	120
Nicola Woollon	121
Hayley Setterfield	121
Joshua Dunne	122

Stacey Nicholls	123
Charlotte Whiting	124
Joanna Strickland	124
Charlotte Oki	125
Michael Hadley	125
Leon Else	126
Michael Carpenter	126
Hayley Wardle	127
Tim McArthur	127
Charlotte White-Perkins	128
Emma How	128
Vicki Golds	129
Paul Beechey	129
Kimberley Page	130
Toni Sabourin	130
Carla Coates	131
Leanne Mitchell	132
Michael Cooper	132
Christopher Waddington	133
Aaron Rouse	133
Natalie Stott	134
Helen Lally	134
Louanna Coltham	135
Danielle Cook	135
Terry Lane	136
Hayley Jehle	136
Douglas Sinclair	137
Laura Moore	138
Hollie Marsh	139
Tabitha Martin	139
Alexandra Sabourin	140
Hannah Skull	140
Kayley Moore	141
Ben Catt	142
Oliver Donohoe	143
Elizabeth Kilbee	144
Kieran Morris	145
Stephen Stroud	146

	Alan Dewsnap	146
	Jason Wasley	147
	Lucy Hughes	147
	Tom Horn	148
	Cheryl Stace	148
Hayes School		
	Jefferson Regan	149
	Laura Draper	149
	Helen McCredie	150
	David Simmons	150
	Alex Wheatley	151
	Katharine Christopher	152
	Martin Sharpe	153
	Daniel Shears	154
	Amy Pierce	155
	Terry West	156
Holy Trinity College		
	Sobiya Yogeswaran	156
	Caroline Mound	157
	Leonie MacCann	158
	Nancy Sullivan	159
	Stephanie Aungier	160
	Juliet Newth	161
	Jade Simmonds	162
	Ekene Oboko	163
	Lydia Burocchi	164
	Charlotte Jacks	164
	Sarah Mantle	165
King's School		
	Scott Tucker	166
	Edward Kevis	166
	Michael Labrou	167
	Rebecca Fenton	168
	Marvin Kissoon	168
	Thomas Hourigan	169

Charlie Beslee	170
Edward Gutierrez	171
Jumana Abbas	172
Scott Goatham	173

Langley Park School For Boys

Stephen Slatter	174
Tom Reeve	175
David Stevens	176
Mark Skinner	177
Robbie Houghton	178
Peter Stylianou	179
Richard Mitchell	180
Samuel Fox	181

Marjorie McClure Special School

Jennifer Hicks	182
Mark Cayzer	182
Laura Buxton	183
Caraline Thompson	183
Michael Waters	184
Matthew Brockhouse	184
Charli Wheeler	185

Newstead Wood School

Sarah Broadbent	185
Zoe Tovell	186
Laura Brown	186
Eleanor Swift	187
Kit Hopkin	188
Saskia Stevenson	188
Kirsty Brett	189
Sarah Burnett	190
H B Bryant	191
Clare Lambourne	191
Stephanie Matthews	192

Rainham Mark Grammar School
> Stacey Martin   193

Rainham School For Girls
> Sonia Sharma   194
> Faye Pinkney   194
> Sharon Wills   195
> Lisa Michael   195
> Debbie Thornton   196
> Kira Hammond   196
> Kylie Hancock   197
> Katie Dearden   197
> Emma Henthorn   198
> Nicola Palfreyman   198
> Alisa Webb   199
> Emily Edwards   199
> Michelle Ambrose   200
> Stacey Moore   200
> Lisa Ash   201
> Emma Johnson   201
> Laura Lodge   202
> Kerry King   202
> Nikki Jones   203
> Charlotte White   204
> Victoria Belcher   204
> Stephanie Chaplin   205
> Rachel Lamonby   206
> Lucy Brisley   207
> Jodie Stringer   208
> Jennifer Burton   208
> Abigail Richardson   209
> Sarah Newman   209
> Claire Geary   210
> Holly Newland   210
> Natalie Wyatt   211
> Dana-Jade Carter   212
> Jade Dover   212
> Victoria Grace Smith   213

Aqsa Khan	214
Ruth Gilby	214
Amber Khawaja	215
Sarah-Dee King	216
Kylie Austin	216
Claire Green	217
Rebecca Miles	217
Hannah Grant	218
Zia Whitehead	218
Tanya Horne	219
Shelley Collings	219
Sarah Sloan	220
Rachel Finniss	220
Katy McCutcheon	221
Zoey Orford	221
Michaela Whittaker	222
Samantha Kittredge	222
Hayley Bodkin	223
Lauren Ramson	223
Katie Hobbs	224
Lauren Hendry	224
Carla White	225
Nicola Carver	226
Montana Burch	226
Natasha Ford	227
Leanne Lawson	228
Nicola Wall	228
Natalie Thomson	229
Charlotte Pullen	230
Ashleigh Crozier	230
Becky Creavin	231
Katie Christy	231
Hannah Jordan	232
Laura Mittoo	232
Natalie Coker	233
Elisabeth Martin	234
Leanne Friday	234
Stacey Purcell	235

Kelly Reavill	236
Francesca Miseldine	236
Kirandeep Basi	237
Sarah Grimes	238
Sian Olsen	238
Lauren A'Court	239
Chloe Dungey	240
Claire Casterton	240
Corinne Walden	241
Kirsty McDougall	241
Amy Sterba	242
Amy Kisby	242
Gemma Cole	243
Erica Wilson	243
Emma Pollett	244
Rachel Toombs	244
Kelly Bessell	245
Samantha Louise Binfield	245
Colette Pascal	246
Laura Harley	246
Suzanne Mills	247
Claire Louise Webb	247
Laura Hanniford	248
Gemma Turner	248
Louise Grant	249
Amanda Conquest	250
Katrina Gordon	250
Alyshia Abramian	251
Zoe Newman	251
Sheona Walsh	252
Tosin Temitope Odubanjo	252
Lea Harrington	253
Melissa Cass	253
Sophie Jimenez	254
Leanne Britton	254
Rachel Hicks	255
Naomi Morrow	255
Hayley Castle	256

	Emily Martin	256
	Jennie Dodds	256
	Martyne Wheeler	257
	Gemma Dicker	257
	Grace Gallacher	258
	Joanne Sargent	258
	Sophia Tuck-Brown	259
	Trudi Wallis	259
	Gillian Pain	260
	Carla Smith	260
Rowhill School		
	Amy Wilmot	261
	Dean Wright	261
	Emma Davies	262
	David Peach & Simon Knapp	263
	Jamie Taylor	263
	Sharon Oakley	264
St Anthony's Special School, Margate		
	Michael Carey	264
	Georgina Parker	265
	Chevy Crompton	266
St Mary & St Joseph's School, Sidcup		
	Corinne Hastings	267
	Katie Edwardes	267
	Nick Smith	268
	Joanna Gallardo	269
	Danika McDonagh	269
	David Beattie	270
	Charlie Sivell	271
	Clare Black	272
	Scott Fry	272
	Paul Husbands	273
	David Gerrard	274
	Sarah Collins	274
	Rebecca Pett	275

Katie Faurie	276
Sarah Cumings	276
James Tristram Smith	277
Stephen Mullan	278
Gareth Pritchard	278
Anna Woodcock	279
Elina Theodoulou	280
Sean Funnell	280
William Lovell	281
Gregory Walker	282
Daniel Dill	282
Emma Duggan	283
Hollie Langley	283
Anucha Forbes	284
Kesha Toussaint	284
Fern Fitzgerald	285
Paul Cumings	286
Danielle McGoldrick	286
Zoe Fernandes	287
Dee Robinson	288
Siobhan O'Neill	288
Nicholas Thomas	289
Michael McGlone	290
Ingrid Elad	290
Leigh-Anne Morrison	291
Luke Oxlade	291
Zoe Purpuri	292
Jemma Gillis	292
Simon Northwood	293
Kirsty Lake	294
Nicky Singh	294
Chris Carmichael	295
Thomas Ford	296
Laura Finn	296
Carla Cunningham	297

The King Ethelbert School
- Philip Crompton — 297
- Michael Hilton — 298
- Simon Smith-Robbie — 298
- Darren Oxborrow — 299
- Natalie Baker — 300
- Lee Joiner — 300
- Daniel Farrier — 301
- Joanne Lamb — 302
- Steven Lloyd — 302
- Claire Lewis — 303
- Lauren Pointer — 304
- Joanne Gough — 305
- Leeroy Fairhurst — 305
- James Lee — 306
- Hannah Swinton — 306
- Shaun Jarman — 307
- Claire Westcott — 308
- Kelly Davenport — 308
- Michael Helder — 309
- Emma Hamlington — 310
- Lauren Kidd — 310
- Simon Hale — 311

Thomas Aveling School
- Cassie Provan — 311
- Matthew Peskett — 312
- Kerrie Lee — 312
- Steve Mashiter — 313

The Poems

THE ESCAPE

I'm starting to yelp,
So now I need some help,
I am in danger, there was a stranger
Who took me away today.
He was tired and weak,
So he fell asleep,
And then I ran away,
So now I'm free
Cos I found a key
And nothing's worrying me.

Tom Luck (11)

TERRIBLE TORNADOES

It burst out of the atmosphere,
Bringing sorrow, bringing fear,
Forecast tells us it's on its way,
Will it strike night or day,
Or will it just pass away?
If it does not pass you by,
You soon realise if you're in the eye of the storm,
First you hear the eerie silence,
Muted by nature's violence.
Then as if an evil demon's nature lets loose its savage beast,
Undercover people fear, why has it hit here?
Ripping up trees, destroying homes,
Mother Nature is a danger, at her worst she's a curse.
As people wake, they fear, what was the damage they could hear
Cars on roofs, trees in roads, that's the way tornadoes go.
This is the damage everyone feared,
Can this be replaced by the human race?

J Brincat (11)
Borden Grammar School

FUTURE TIMES

Will all the streets be paved with gold?
And filled with people noble and bold?
Will it be dirty, dark and dim,
With robots controlling everything?
Will we destroy this beautiful Earth?
And plunge all we have into darkness and dearth?
Will evolution be reborn,
Or all of Earth be torn and scorn?
Will an ice-age cover all with snow?
Some of these things we'll never know.
Will a volcano cover all with ash,
Or maybe a comet will come down with a crash?
Will we survive Earth's hideous end?
And then live on Mars - our friend?
Future only conceals,
What we want it to reveal.

Stephen Wood (14)
Borden Grammar School

IF (WHAT A BEAUTIFUL CREATURE I'D BE)

If I could soar through the clouds like a bird,
Above the land and the sea,
It would certainly be absurd,
But what a beautiful creature I'd be.

If I could dig down in the soil of Mother Earth,
All the amazing sights I'd see,
I would dig right out of my turf,
But what a beautiful creature I'd be.

If I could swim in the deep, wide ocean,
And to all secrets I was the key,
I would swim fast in a flawless motion,
But what a beautiful creature I'd be.

If I could disappear into parallel time,
And all the angels would adore me,
I'd drink Bacardi and lime,
But what a beautiful creature I'd be.

Shawn Tyrrell (14)
Borden Grammar School

SPRING

The sunshine thaws the snow-white frost,
And brings back warm days we thought we'd lost.
Rivers start to trickle, their ice melting fast,
Hooray the spring we thought was gone has come back at last.
Snow turns to white slush, gathering in the hollows,
We gather outside, arms held wide to welcome all the swallows.

Buds pop out on bush and tree,
My, what a wondrous sight to see.
Flowers open just like new pearls,
While children play without a care in the world.
Grass uncurls beneath our feet
And snow folds up like a big white sheet.

Frisky lambs on hillsides steep,
Like to prance and sleep and leap.
Bluebells bloom with beauty untold,
Awakening from a sleep in the cold.
Hibernating creatures uncurl and yawn,
Waking up to a bright spring dawn.

Ben Wright (11)
Borden Grammar School

NOISES IN SITUATIONS

The guitar may play that twangy note,
The glockenspiel goes ping, ping.
The tuba may blow as a raspberry does,
And then, the flute starts to sing.

The string band will play a waltzing tune,
They go zing and carry along.
The brass band may go, tiddly pom,
While playing a marching song.

When you sit on an ice-cream it goes squish and squelch,
On a thistle, you cry out in pain.
You scream when you sit on a nettle that stings,
But your cries are often in vain.

The mongrel will run around, barking like mad,
The mouse will squeak due to fear.
The sleek, slim cats will rummage around,
Purring, so we can hear.

The clock will chime, at each every hour,
For example, just like Big Ben.
Twenty four hours, just in one day,
Then doing it all over again.

Matthew Horder (11)
Borden Grammar School

WHAT WILL I BECOME?

As I look into the future
And see distant days bringing
Fortune to some,
I glance into time and ask myself
The simple question, what will I become?

I can see it clearer now,
When I grow older,
But on lonely, wet evenings with nothing to do,
Somehow I wish,
The future could be happy and a lot bolder too.

Jamie White (13)
Borden Grammar School

THE WAITING GAME

Almost there
Only seven negligible days left.
At first it's just sheer anger and pain,
Then,
As the target gets ever nearer,
They seem to grow longer.
All you can think about is the painstaking wait ahead,
The day draws closer and closer,
You're feeling frustrated,
Anxiety,
Excitement and pain,
But out of all of this stress,
In all of its grace and beauty,
The day rolls in,
A year of saving,
A month of scouring the shops,
A fortnight of decision,
A week of waiting,
Now,
My new bike beckons.

Gregory Brissenden (13)
Borden Grammar School

BROKEN DREAMS

As the hands move round the numbered face,
Always travelling so slow in this boring place,
Why can't I be in a paradise of my own?
Like on a sandy beach all alone,
Or on a deserted cliff standing upon a ledge,
Daring myself to jump off the closing edge,
And land in a world harmless and caring,
Where people are warm, kind and sharing.
For there, no one can hurt my feelings in such ways,
As people do in these lonely, hate-filled days.
They build up my hopes so they can tear them down,
They break my heart, people turn against me all around.
So why can't I be in a world of my own?
Where no one will ever, ever be shown.

James Palmer (13)
Borden Grammar School

MY FAMILY

My family make me very cross,
My mum thinks that she is the boss.
My dad always moans and complains,
When I go near the garden canes.

My family are really horrid,
They make me eat raw porridge.
My sister is a big, big pain,
But I always get the blame.

Could this be what my family will be,
In the year two thousand and three!

Christopher Dean (13)
Borden Grammar School

Autumn

Leaves of brown, red and gold,
no longer on the tree they hold.
The sun no longer stands out bold,
as the autumn wind comes in cold.

Birds migrate far away,
as all around the trees rock and sway.
Animals start their harvest days,
finding food in different ways.

The summer moves towards its end,
winter's just around the bend.
Days are cold and full of dew,
autumn falls on me and you.

Liam Scarfe (11)
Borden Grammar School

The Future Of An Over Eighteen Sign

At the present
I'm not seen,
I'm not known,
By people under and over eighteen.

In the future
I'll be noticed,
I'll be law
It will be posted.

I'll be recognised
I'll be seen,
People will be aware
I'm for over eighteens!

Adam Mullins (13)
Borden Grammar School

LITTLE TIM AND ANDREW

There was once a boy called Andrew,
Who thought bullying would never go,
Until it got to him,
And he bought a little bulldog, called Tim.
Then one boy was filled with hate,
And was served, at dinner, on a plate!
However, one day, Andrew lost him,
And nearly drowned looking for him.
Then ten years later, when he had given up hope,
He found Tim was now owned by the Pope!
He went to this Pope, bold and strong,
When someone struck the gong,
'Let the argument commence!' someone yelled,
And was punched once while he was held.
'Give my dog back, you bitter pill,'
'No, I will tell my guards to kill.'
'If so, you are not kind,'
'So what? I will tell my guards to whip your behind!'
'Oh sure, where are your guards?'
'In the audience, dressed as bards!'
'And I guess you haven't noticed I nabbed my Tim,'
'I've had enough. Guards, whip him!'
'Not a chance, sire,
Or should I say Fat Squire!'
So Andrew held Tim high,
Goodness knows why
Where he stood proud and powerful,
While the Pope acted cowerful.
Then the two went home until they died,
And nobody saw the Pope as he tried to hide.

Martin Spokes (11)
Borden Grammar School

THE ALIENS

The alien spaceship up in the sky,
Squeals and bleeps as it goes by,
It stops and lands in my backyard,
It's shiny and metal and must be quite hard.
It gently lands on the rabbit pen,
It flies afar, and then back again.
I must admit, it's quite bizarre,
To see these things that come from Mars.
A crack of light shines from the ship,
Now I'm scared, I bite my lip.
The hatch of the ship opens slow,
To reveal three aliens, all in a row.
One is short, one is tall,
One is fat and starts to fall,
He falls out of his ship and rolls to my feet,
I hold out a shaky hand, ready to greet.
Two black holes look up at my face,
I feel pretty weak and my heart starts to race.
He stands up on four legs and holds out a hand,
It is slimy and rubbery and really dark tanned.
Its head, the size of a dinner dish,
The black holes stare and say 'I wish.'
Fat and thin came marching in,
To the garden that we stood within.
They retreat to the ship from which they came,
I say goodbye, it's quite a shame.
'Sorry, repairs,' they said,
It was fun, this night of fright,
I see them zoom off at the speed of light.

Sean Parker (11)
Borden Grammar School

CANNABIS ALERT!

Don't legalise the green smoke,
If Labour do,
They'll be taken for a joke!

Don't legalise the green smoke,
And terrorise,
The normal folk!

Don't legalise the green smoke,
On its air,
We will choke!

If we did,
It would be dippy.

I don't want to be no hippy!

Aden Philpott (13)
Borden Grammar School

TOUGH

What does it mean to be tough?

Some say it is a person who is strong,
Or that they can take a blow.
Maybe they are feared by all?

What does it mean to be tough?

Some think that it is a person who is afraid of being weak,
Or that a blow does hurt them but they are afraid to show it.
Maybe they are scared of not fitting in?

Maybe, to be tough is to pretend.

Peter Harris (13)
Borden Grammar School

TOUGH

It's hard being tough,
You have to look rough.
Being tough,
Makes me look like a scruff.

You have to look cool,
Misbehave at school.
You can't do what you want to do,
Because people are watching you.

It's hard being tough,
You have to look rough.
Being tough,
Makes me look a scruff.

You push people over for fun,
The teachers think you're dumb.
You can't get a girl,
The teachers give you hell.

It's hard being tough,
You have to look rough.
Being tough,
Makes me look a scruff.

You lose a fight,
Pick on someone your own height.
You've got a black eye,
Nose as high as the sky.

It's hard being tough.

A J Manning (14)
Borden Grammar School

FUTURE

In the future we are all going to die,
Then to the world we say goodbye,
Dead and buried and laid to rest,
Six feet under in a wooden chest.

No more birds singing in the trees,
No more buzzing from bumblebees,
No more anything for us to see,
This sounds like somewhere I do not want to be.

No more colours, bright and loud,
No more peacocks, big and proud,
Even though I've passed away,
I expect people will remember me in their own way.

The way I acted,
The things I did,
How I walked,
The way I talked.

These are the things that made me me!

Jason Mathew Willmore (16)
Borden Grammar School

FUTURE'S DESTINY

How will the future be?
Full of hope for humanity?
Will the world be free of hurt?
Will the world be full of dirt?

I hope the future will be bright,
I hope that we all do things right.
All of our troubles we have to mend,
Try to bring world hunger to an end.

All the world may live in peace,
But all world wars have to cease.
All evil dictators have to stop,
For our civilisation to reach the top.

Will we meet aliens from outer space,
Who help us to unify the human race?
All of our future we do not know,
So into the wilderness we must go.

Garry Walmsley (17)
Borden Grammar School

THE FUTURE

Nobody knows what the future will hold,
Everybody is expecting so much,
Will it live up to its expectations,
And please everybody so.

Will technology improve,
Or will we have flying cars?
Will robots take over man?
Only the future will tell.

Will we have speaking robot maids,
Or an automated kitchen?
Will we not need to work, or
Will we have to work harder?

The future is unknown,
Only time will tell.
What we are expecting,
Only the future will tell.

Scott Teague (17)
Borden Grammar School

PEACE?

In the future everyone will live peacefully,
Animals are no longer hunted for fun or sport,
   The world lives together in perfect harmony,
Twenty years ago the last war was fought,
   Afterwards nobody wanted to fight again,
Peace was finally successful for once,
   Poverty, famine and disease were gone - there was no more pain.

Pollution is no longer a problem too,
   Scientists have worked together to solve the clues,
The ozone layer has been made fine again,
   Waste is sent out into the sun to burn,
Trees have been planted all over the place,
   The world is green once more,
Wildlife is thriving alongside the human race.

   Hopefully this peace will last forever,
I don't want my family to suffer,
   It will not last if we don't stick together,
However it all depends on the young,
   We need to teach them the importance of peace!

Nick Brend (14)
Borden Grammar School

EL FUTURE

Next week, I may be sitting here,
Two days, I may be writing here,
Next year, I may be thinking here,
Tomorrow, I may not be here!

People may not be wearing anything,
No, no, no,
Cos of global warming,
Yeah, yeah, yeah.

A hundred mile an hour faster,
I'm talking about the speed,
Yeah that's right, the speed man,
The speed of music man.

Why do people always talk,
Talk about the past,
Why talk about the past?
You can't go back, you only go forward!

Lewis Peter Smith (16)
Borden Grammar School

THE FUTURE

On the Earth, when the present now is past,
Robots and gadgets skid around,
Like children on ice,
Then in the air.
Fast vehicles skim the buildings,
One by one,
By floating platforms, like steps to homes,
Which are used in Senate
Man and robot have reached Pluto.

To go on the roads, on the ground,
Is now a punishable offence,
Aliens have been proved to exist.
Buildings which are made of steel
And the pickety world with new wonders.
The electric escalators transporting people,
From place to place.

The future is here
So let's begin to fit the role.

Andrew Owens (11)
Borden Grammar School

HOPEFUL

Hey man, come over here,
Shed me a tear,
And I'll believe in you.

Hey man, the future's warm,
Let the fire,
Slowly eat you.

Have you ever seen this black before?
Well carry on and I'll show you some more.

Hey man, it's cold outside,
Icy winds,
Blow doubt in your mind.

Was all you wanted something to call your own?
And is the candle of hope burning too low?

(Please listen to the future's dream;
Save yourself!
The bleakest hour has been.)

Shane Dowle (16)
Borden Grammar School

THE FUTURE

The 21st century, what will it bring?
Will it be cars running on electricity,
Or will it be cars that fly,
With motorways high in the sky?

The 21st century, what will it bring?
Robots in factories replacing us,
With robots at home doing our work,
Or will it all be done with a big smirk?

The 21st century, what will it bring?
Computers that run at the speed of light
And buying products on TV from America.
Will we be able to watch a sport's event of our choice on TV?
And will we be able to swim in a clean, deep, blue sea?

The 21st century, what will it bring?
Gadgets for absolutely everything,
We will just have to wait and see
Perhaps nothing will change just like you and me.

Darren Nokes (16)
Borden Grammar School

THE FUTURE

No one knows what the future holds,
There have been many tales told,
About what will happen in the future,
Nobody knows what is around the corner
A lifetime of love or an hour in a sauna.

Some people predict what will happen next,
Will we have big laser guns?
Will we eat only chocolate buns?
Will we colonise outer space?
Will we discover alien race?

When will the world end?
What is around the next bend?
Will we invent a really big boat?
Will we be ruled by intelligent goats?

Nobody knows what the future holds.

Matthew Murdoch (13)
Borden Grammar School

FUTURE

No one quite knows,
and it shows,
the plan, fate,
and monotonous debate,
as to the happenings of the distant present.

The world's going to end,
people are going to evolve,
and one day may will effectively be extinct;
but how do we know?

The question of mankind's nature to destroy themselves,
could it really be true?
Because that would mean that the future holds
the dirt of man - on nature's shoe.

No one quite knows,
and it shows,
the plan, fate
and monotonous debate,
as to the happenings of the distant present.

Terry Seager
Borden Grammar School

ROALD DAHL

Roald Dahl was his name,
Naughtiness was his game,
When he was young and daring,
He was very good at scaring,
He scared away the teacher,
He scared away the cook,
But none of this was nearly as good as his 'boy' book.

When he was older and more mature,
The world and Germany had a great war,
He fought for country with his heart,
The stories of this became a well-earned art.

He was a very bright and funny man,
If he couldn't write a book, no one can!

David Taylor (13)
Borden Grammar School

ALIEN

What would you do if an alien walked down the street?
Is he the kind of person you would like to meet?
With his long green fingers and no hair.
Would everybody stare at him or just not care?
What would you do if he knocked on the door?
Would you punch and kick him until he felt sore?
Do you think he would act like us?
I think surely he really must.
Would he walk?
Would he talk?
Could he see?
Fly like a bee?
No one knows the answers except for me.
I can walk.
I can talk.
I can see and fly like a bee
But what about humans?
Are they clever?
Can they make metal out of leather
I don't know,
I don't care
And by the way what is hair?

Christopher Payne (13)
Borden Grammar School

FUTURE ECHOES

Black holes and wormholes once unobserved,
With telescopes brought within sight,
Exploration advances once concealed,
Roam universe faster than light,

Computer technology once unfriendly,
Possibilities now without end,
Boldly explored every aspect of life,
The ultimate word now just 'send',

Man's termination that was once expected
Cut short with its approaching,
The quest for eternal youth,
Never more to be encroaching,

Cancer and AIDS once diseases unsolved,
Have cures never imagined before,
The plagues of mankind with misery severe,
Will threaten and frighten no more,

Where impending destruction was once on our minds,
The laughter and joy of freeness of time,
No more to be stressing and living in fear,
The time of the end is coming so near.

Matthew Mawson (13)
Borden Grammar School

TOMORROW

When my mum says 'Clean your room,'
I say 'I'll do it tomorrow.'
When my dad says 'Wash the car,'
I say 'I'll do it tomorrow,'
When my brother says 'Go to the park,'
I say 'I'll do it tomorrow.'
Tomorrow never comes.

When I say 'Mum, where's my washing?'
She says 'I'll do it tomorrow.'
When I say 'Dad, sort out my money,'
He says 'I'll do it tomorrow.'
Tomorrow never comes.

Anthony Sage (15)
Borden Grammar School

ENTANGLED IN A WHIRLWIND

Those voices still haunt me, as clear as water locked in my mind.
It's as though I'm a prisoner to them, they've captured me.
No, I can't be a slave to them, I must be strong and resist,
It's as though there's a message hidden within,
Is it good or is it bad, or is there just no rhyme at all?
Why did this torture begin?
Was it to warn me, scare me or just for a joke?

Ha, ha, ha, ha, you are a fool, you have entered our world of fire,
Your mind is now nothing but a mass of burning debris.
You are our prisoner, caught for all time and eternity.

No, he's not your prisoner, he's mine!
He's the last lost lamb of my precious flock
So now I will return him to safety, from your tangled snare of gloom.

I'm free! Free of the whirlwind which fixed me like a straightjacket.
Hope, hope is all you need so remember hope is the key.
The thought all whirlwinds die sometime, gave me hope.
I concentrated, put my mind at ease with thoughts of good,
Then the snare was released, the whirlwind passed the horizon
                                                      of my mind.

Richard Barling (14)
Borden Grammar School

LOOKING UP

The stars are out tonight,
A lone shadow stands looking up,
Hidden from the scene he knows,
The endless opportunities stretch,
A lake of fantasies where reality grows.
For all that he has run through,
Head on, as a deer in a park,
He knows he has been flying high,
But now the ground is back.

The breeze has come tonight,
The cooling force can penetrate,
To lift up what's to come,
When change has transformed him,
When these feelings overrun
Although the chapter's read now,
The book goes on and on,
For soon, new stories will unfold,
With the emptiness felt, all gone.

The sky is clear tonight,
At last, the clouds have seen their place,
The future all seems clear in space,
It's looking up,
And he's smiling.

Phil Simpson (16)
Borden Grammar School

GLOBAL WARMING

Here I am in 2050,
People suffering more and more from skin cancers,
Water levels rising,
The Greenhouse Effect trapping heat,
People suffering from dehydration,
Acid rain eroding statues, cliffs and much more.

The press said we would suffer,
The news told us to do something about it,
The Government spoke encouraging words to cyclists, walkers
And the concerned public,
Scientists discovered ways to prevent the effect.

Still we persist in using aeroplanes and buses,
Public transport is insufficient for time,
People using cars just to go small distances,
People grow lazier.

What will become of the world?
Will it be an extreme planet of heat?
Will anything ever again be seen here?
Will the universe be empty?
Will something save us from extreme heat?

At least cyclists are still keen,
A lot of walkers still stroll around,
Joggers still run in pairs,
Families still walk their dogs.

William Lay (13)
Borden Grammar School

DEVASTATION

Move, run to anywhere you can,
Because India has just declared war on Pakistan,
All of the countries have chosen their sides,
But did they have to do it out of stupid pride?

Hurry, we haven't got all day, you hear the people saying,
Some people are just standing around praying,
The end of the world is upon us,
Why did those two countries have to kick up such a fuss?

Well now the bombs have been dropped,
Not long now before all will be stopped.
Some people think they will be okay,
But the radiation will get them to their dismay.

I feel the people have had it so bad,
Why did the military have to go so mad?
All we wanted was a peaceful planet,
Did we ever think we would get it?

Matthew Wood (16)
Borden Grammar School

CYNICAL FUTURE

Not the past and not the present,
Tomorrow could be good, tomorrow could be pleasant,
Time ticks one way, forward, not back,
Here I am, a needle in a haystack.

I have my doubts, I have my worries,
Roads overrun with cars and lorries,
Pollution chokes the Earth with smog and flame,
Everyone knows the fat cats are there to blame.

Man hath conquered and destroyed,
Dictators cruel with armies deployed,
People are tortured and oppressed,
But the west is rich and is blessed.

Tomorrow is another day,
Helpless we stand in dismay,
We must look forward with warm hearts and be well,
The Earth is doomed, may we rot in hell!

Robert Wisniewski (16)
Borden Grammar School

THE MILLENNIUM

Who knows what might happen?
The world might end
The computer's round the bend.

So many things have been marked
You can get jewellery, stationery, all kinds of things
You have always had people who sang
It all may go off with a bang.

People will be celebrating
Pubs and clubs will be full
Drunks acting like a fool.

The next day people will feel terrible
Wish they had never done it.
It may seem just a normal day
People acting in a normal way.

Who knows what it will be
We will just have to wait and see.

Giles Gabriel (15)
Borden Grammar School

Napoleonic Lesson

In the year two thousand and one,
The Napoleonic studies begun,
They made up a rhyme,
For a great battle in time,
They knew what it meant,
And this is how it went.

Sharpe and his squad were cleaning Harper's gun,
When they heard the bugle sound and began to run,
They went into Wellington's tent,
To hear the message that was sent.

They had to meet up with a platoon,
They had to steal some gold doubloon,
They had to attack a French outpost,
Which was situated by the coast.

They packed and went on their way,
They should arrive by midday,
On the way they met some Spanish,
They beat them up and told them to vanish.

When they arrived they smelt gunpowder,
They started to shoot which made the sound louder,
There were bloodcurdling screams,
While Sharpe yelled out the teams.

Sharpe hacked his way through the men,
He had found the French treasure den,
He lit the dynamite,
This would give him a fright,
They ran as fast as they could go,
The bang was like a firework shop.

So that was how it was told,
Later on the story was sold.

Stuart Green (14)
Borden Grammar School

WHAT THE FUTURE MAY HOLD

What the future may hold,
can sometimes never be told.
One can never look into the future
because of its mystery,
one can only look back into history.
The future can hold good or bad,
which could make you happy or sad.
If the future holds failure or success,
one must look back in interest.
The future one must wait,
like fishing without bait.
The future can only be explained,
when the day of reckoning comes.
But just like the *pretence*
one must wait for the future
with the utmost patience.

Charles Ayre (16)
Borden Grammar School

STACKMEISTER

I breath into the mellow night
not a man or woman in sight
the pain in my knees intensifies
as I try to cycle with all my might.

My wheels will go over all the lumps
my suspension will soak up all the humps
but none of that is enough
to stop me falling as I hit a bump.

I fall down the mountainside
a sharp pain hits my thigh
why didn't I see the bump?
There must have been something in my eye.

As I crawl into A and E
the sharp pain progresses to my knee
I see them amputate my leg
I could not notice, the doctor had very nice teeth.

Weiran Zhang (13)
Borden Grammar School

FUTURE SPORT

There will be football, and cricket and athletics too,
There will be plenty of sports for people to do.
You could play rugby on Venus and snooker on Mars,
Just imagine, nowhere will be too far.

Football's a sport which involves a lot of kicking,
Football's a sport which involves a lot of thinking.
The aim is to score against the opposition,
But to do this you have to be in a good position.

Running's a sport in which you need a lot of pace,
This is because all the athletes race.
All the athletes hope to finish the race,
But most of all they want to come first place.

Even though wrestling's not a proper sport,
I would definitely give it higher than naught.
It's exciting to watch and I could view it all day,
But some people consider it as a drama play.

James Ashford (13)
Borden Grammar School

THE WAR

All those who lost their feet and hands,
Don't want to battle anymore.
Everybody in other and different lands,
Hate to see anymore war.

Lots of people suffering through loss of homes,
Don't want to battle anymore.
Lots of people with missing legs and bones,
Hate to see anymore war.

We have to kill and slaughter some more,
Don't want to battle anymore.
Just to overcome all the wars,
Hate to see anymore war.

The next generation shouldn't start any war,
Because it will lead to violence and more.
We shouldn't carry on with this pain and gore,
So it would be better if we don't repeat war.

Marcus Patrick Newing (14)
Borden Grammar School

A Bloke's Sunday

He woke up late,
Late for the game,
He'll have to be quick to meet his mate,
Who is very lame.

He got to the match
And played up front.
He jumped in a mud patch
And looked like a punk.

He ran with might
To get the ball,
He kicked it like light
As someone shouted goal.

He dived on the floor
As his celebration,
And surely the match ball
Was for his presentation.

The trophy was his,
One more for collection,
And he could now kiss
The trophy with a lot of affection.

He went to the pub
For an afternoon pint,
He started a scrub
Which led to a fight.

Carl O'Neill (13)
Borden Grammar School

FUTURE VOICES

In the future there will be flying cars,
And people will be living on Mars,
In exchange aliens will live among us,
And nobody will cause a fuss,
Because we'll accept them as one of us.

They have ended war,
And created peace on Earth, I'm sure.

Humans will have conquered space,
And on every planet will be the world leader's face.

In the future there will be an end to famine,
And all our faces we will be cramming,
With genetically engineered foods.

In the future we won't need prisons,
Because there won't be any booze or drugs,
Thus preventing intoxicated thugs.

In the future they will be contented,
With the new world *they* invented,
They will have fixed the *ozone*,
And saved the rainforests,
Purified the oceans,
Replaced some trees,
And cured all forms of disease,
Then they'll look back at us in the 20th century,
And laugh at how foolish we were!

William Tyrrell (13)
Borden Grammar School

THE BUG

Who cares about the millennium, not me!
I can tell you that.
Everybody's got the Millennium Bug,
I couldn't care less.
I just shrug every time someone asks what I'm going to do.
Maybe I could spend the night with you
And we could watch TV and have an early night.
That sounds good, ya think?
It would be hard to try and really enjoy the night.
We get one, just one chance to get some fun,
Which would be really saddening if we got it wrong and messed up.
It will only be a phenomenal anticlimax,
You'll see,
We'll see,
Won't we?

Andrew Dickson (14)
Borden Grammar School

ERUTUF GNIEB A MROW

My object for tomorrow is to tunnel for as far as I can,
This will begin at the crack of dawn.
I will know when the morning comes,
The birds will awake me as usual.
Their tiny feet sound like elephants stampeding upon my roof.
Perhaps it would rain, which would start my day,
Then I could go to the outer world,
For some fresh air, which would be nice.
Isn't life so complicated being a worm,
Because you just don't know what tomorrow will bring.

Kris Forshaw (13)
Borden Grammar School

WHAT WILL THE FUTURE BE LIKE?

Will there be hovercars?
And how will they fly?
Or will there be robots,
That don't hurt and don't cry?

Will we do anything,
Or nothing at all?
Will we play sports still,
Like hockey and football?

Will we have school, years on,
Or stay at home all day?
Then we won't need teachers,
So they can go away.

Will computers take over,
And replace the writing pen?
If it's gonna happen,
I want to know when.

Will we still have pets,
Or won't we be allowed?
I'm not sure who's against it,
But there must be quite a crowd.

If I was offered the future,
To see what I would do,
I'd probably turn around,
And say 'No thank you.'

Glen Johnson (14)
Borden Grammar School

TECHNOLOGY

In the future will technology rule our lives?
Updated modems and new disc drives.
Will we have a life of our own,
Or will it be ruled by the mobile phone?

Many people have different theories,
Many people have different thoughts.
Many people have different queries,
Some don't care at all.

The computer is a complex machine,
Made of circuits, megabytes, all compact and clean.
Many a house contain these devices,
They come in a whole range of shapes and sizes.

So since these creations have been invented,
The demand for them has extended.
So no wonder people have queries,
Or concocting strange theories of today's technology taking over.

Ashley Thomas (13)
Borden Grammar School

THE FUTURE!

What will the future hold for me?
Will they abolish colour,
Or just annihilate burgundy?

Will cars travel up to the stars,
Or will we still be trying to reach Mars?
Will traffic lower immensely,
Or will populations be condensely?

Will there be wacky weapons and guns,
Or will there be robotic mums?
Will food be the same as now,
Or will it be thin and reedy?
And will people's eyes be small and beady?

Will we have made contact with other life forms,
Or will we still use foghorns?

James Gibson (13)
Borden Grammar School

THE ASTEROID

It's coming, the asteroid's coming,
You can see it in the sky
Tearing through the puffy white clouds,
Getting closer, closer, closer.

There will be no tomorrow,
And there will be no more of today
As the asteroid is getting nearer,
It's going to get us all.

All the pain and suffering going on now,
Family's cuddled up, not looking.
Just waiting, waiting and waiting
For the power of the asteroid is too much.

It gets louder and bigger every second,
If only man could live on the moon.
Suppose it's too late for us now,
As the asteroid's getting closer.

Closer, closer, closer, clo . . .

Adam Grigsby (15)
Borden Grammar School

EARTH AND SPACE IN THE FUTURE

In the future, space will be so great,
In the future we will be living on the moon,
Mixing with other life forms.
The Earth will be iced over.
Instead of cars we will have hoverbikes,
Travelling through space at thousands of miles per hour,
The other life forms produce the power.

On the other hand:

We could still be living on Earth,
Where each second there's a death and birth,
Babies born and adults die,
The Earth could be as it is today,
But, maybe, just maybe,
The Earth could be a better place,
Where everybody cares for every race.
Be it men or women, blacks or whites, cats or dogs, cows or frogs.
We could all make the world a better place
For the future.

Michael Evans (15)
Borden Grammar School

THE FUTURE

People will drive floating cars,
We will be covered in ozone scars.
Dogs will live in spaceships,
Rabbits will live on GM pips.

In the future we will live in PCs,
We'll be full of micro fleas.
People's brains will be CD roms,
Their ears will be pom-poms.

People's heads will be tin cans,
Their feet will be frying pans,
We won't hear a sound,
Cos we'll be living underground.

We'll live in cardboard boxes,
And we'll eat run-down foxes.
We won't drink Coca-Cola,
And we'll eat hyper-bola.

Neil Goodhew (13)
Borden Grammar School

A QUESTION ASKED

What will the future be like?
What will it have?
Will it have roads?
Will it have cars?
Will it have planes that soar through the air?
Will it have buildings and houses like now?
What will the future be like?

Will people have jobs?
Will robots be there?
Will I have relatives?
What will they do?
How will they live?
How will they seem?
What will the future be like?

I wish I knew
I wish I could go
I wish I could see what the future will be.

Nathaniel Daniels (16)
Borden Grammar School

FUTURE LIVES

Tomorrow the future
Yesterday's the past.
What can we do
When the years go fast.

Soon it'll be uni,
Then a car,
This will be soon
When the years go fast.

Then I'll have a job,
At the age of thirty.
Then I will earn
A lot of money.

When I get old,
I will get
Weak and tired.
This is in hold
For my long, long future.

Vishal Mistry (14)
Borden Grammar School

FUTURE'S CHILD

The voices,
I hear the voices,
The voices of the future's child.

It cries in pain,
The pain of nothingness,
Nothing but the future's child exists.

No vegetation,
No life,
Nothing.

Is this how it's going to be?
It doesn't answer,
It just cries.

Cries in pain.

Daniel Howard (13)
Borden Grammar School

FUTURE CHILDREN

The voices,
I hear voices,
Voices of those who are dead,
Voices of those who are living,
Voices of those who are not yet born.

The images,
I see images,
Images of lost loved ones,
Images of present loved ones,
Images of future loved ones.

The emotions,
I feel emotions,
Emotions referring to people who have passed away,
Emotions towards those who are living,
Future emotions to unborn children.

Jacob Brown (13)
Borden Grammar School

CHEESE

I hate cheese
I wonder
Will we need it?
Do we need it?
No
It's pointless
In the future will we need cheese?
It's never helped us before
never helped to win our war
Against fat, or anything
It just sits there, what am I to do?
I don't know, neither do you
maybe, in the future we'll find a use for it
but I doubt it.
Is it fun?
No.
Will it be fun?
No.
After all, it's only cheese.
Do we care what happens to it?
I don't, neither do you
unless of course in the future
people like it.

James Loose (15)
Borden Grammar School

THE NEXT FEW DAYS

The future isn't just about the year 2000
It can be about what happens next.
It's not all about the Millennium Dome
Or fireworks and parties,
It's about what you make of it
Whether it's good or bad.

Will there be hovercars and battery powered planes
Or will it all be normal cars and aeroplanes?
Will wars stop and famine stop?
Will poverty be cured and global warming gone?
The way we are going
I can safely say no!

Christopher Beck (13)
Borden Grammar School

MY DAD, MY FUTURE

What you mean to me you'll never know,
The things you have taught me,
The words of wisdom you have given,
The comfort and understanding you have brought me,
The way in which it was given.

You've stood by me through thick and thin,
Believing me,
With trouble I've got myself in.

You're always there to guide me,
And lend a helping hand,
You're always right beside me,
Wherever I may stand.

Your love and kindness will always be remembered,
You're truly a remarkable man,
Helping anyone in whatever way you can.

I will always respect you,
Always trust you,
But most of all,
I will always *love* you.

Luke Auron-Cotton (14)
Borden Grammar School

THE FUTURE COULD BE STRANGE

The future could be so *strange*.
A word meaning odd or *bizarre*,
A fund-raising event held by a *school*,
An institution for educating *pupils*,
The circular opening in the centre of the *eye*,
The ninth letter of the *alphabet*,
A group of symbols for writing a *language*,
The form of communication used by the human *race*,
A competition in which the aim is to *win*,
To receive a *prize*
A token of *victory*,
To defeat one's enemy in *war*,
To argue and *destroy*,
Terminate!

Darren Brown (15)
Borden Grammar School

WORLD WAR III

There will be another war,
Just like the two before,
Only this time the world will come to an end.

Some Eastern country will start it,
And the UK will be part of it,
Until the whole world picks its part to play.

Will it be over land or over politics?
Or will it be over killing like the Serbians did?
Will we see it coming? No we won't!
It will hit the world without anyone knowing
And then the lands will be glowing
Light the bright burning flames of war.

Russell Cope (15)
Borden Grammar School

THE DYING WORLD

When . . . when did it all go wrong,
Too many cars,
Too much pollution,
Too much rubbish.

It's destroyed our world today,
If only they'd stopped and thought,
Just for a minute,
They've got us into all this trouble.

Soon we will be no more,
Lying dying on the floor,
It's all their fault, back in the '90s,
They never thought about us.

Paul Gregory (14)
Borden Grammar School

STATISTIC

Some people have a good future,
Some people don't,
Some people fear their future,
Some people don't.
But the people who do
Still don't know what lies ahead.
Some people know their future,
Some people don't.
Some people have a future,
Some people don't
But what people don't understand
Is that everyone's future
Is a statistic in the government's hand.

Chris Mills (15)
Borden Grammar School

FUTURE VOICES

Millions of miles of barren space
The sun's so near and yet so far
Then suddenly a miracle
About a single yellow star.
A lump of rock it first appears,
But with a unique gift;
Minute lumps of chemicals,
That promise so much life.
The cycles come, the cycles go,
Life takes what it can find.
Then from the apes comes something new
With a great, amazing mind.
Ten thousand short years later,
This animal has spread,
Humanity's great feats abound
The atom split, Earth left behind,
But what else have we done?
Hate and killing, death and war,
Are also our brainchildren.
In just ten thousand short years time
The Earth's resources drained,
Humanity's new age begins,
But is the past behind?
We cannot carry on like this,
Our future must be more
Than what we have now on our Earth:
Starvation, bloodshed, war.
Our future starts with our today,
We can't keep up like this.
To save our race, we must act now,
To give our children future hope.

Adam Britton-Mosley (14)
Borden Grammar School

IN SIXTY YEARS

In sixty years when I'm old and senile,
Will I be able to look back and smile,
Or will I be full of regrets
Knowing I didn't take enough chances or put on enough bets?
Shall I be able to be content,
With a small house and no rent,
Or will I want a flash car,
And a big house with my own private bar?
Will I sit and talk about the war,
Which I fought in and lost good friends and much more?
Shall I be worrying about Third World poverty,
Or will I not let it bother me?
Who knows what the future holds,
I must just enter it and be bold.

Neil James Haffenden (14)
Borden Grammar School

THE FUTURE OF OLD AGE

All this talk of getting old,
It's getting me down,
Like a cat in a bag,
Waiting to drown,
My time is coming round.

But I know the future holds many keys,
Like the year 2020 when we are living under the sea.
The time will come to say goodbye,
When everyone is living high up in the sky.

So that's the end of our life today,
But tomorrow will be yet another day.

James Stickens (14)
Borden Grammar School

TOMORROW NEVER COMES

Once it was yesterday, now it's today
But will tomorrow ever come.
No, it's just too far away,
We just cannot catch it, it's always on the run!

We always can't wait,
For tomorrow to come
But when we get near it,
It just seems to run!

Yesterday was quite sunny
Yesterday was fun
Today was quite funny
Tomorrow, tomorrow please do not run!

I can't wait until tomorrow
Till I go out and play
I just cannot wait
Tomorrow please come!

Simon Meeks (15)
Borden Grammar School

OBLIVION

Oblivion,
The annihilation.
For each and every one of us,
The end of everything we know.
The predetermined future fate
Of all things,
Living and synthetic.
A major constant in our universe.

Oblivion,
The demise.
A siren call that heralds doom.
For the dinosaur, the Dodo and our relatives
The fiery phoenix of time.
With teeth and talons that rends our flesh,
And in years to come it will be our flesh.
To hear the siren call of
Oblivion.

Chris Bassett (15)
Borden Grammar School

THEY DROP ONCE A YEAR!

They drop once a year,
And they're not so dear,
You guessed it, they're conkers,
Everybody is bonkers about conkers.

They're small and round,
And are less than a pound,
But there are some much larger,
And to some, they are better than lager.

My sister, Daisy,
Who is so crazy,
Loves all conkers,
Which drive her completely bonkers.

Samuel Luckhurst (11)
Borden Grammar School

TOMORROW

What is tomorrow?
I'll tell you what tomorrow is;
Tomorrow is just another day like yesterday
and the day before that and the day before that.

But what will be different about tomorrow?
What new information will I learn?
Will I learn the name of a planet, a mathematical theorem or what?

But tomorrow is going to be pretty much the same as yesterday.
I'll get up and go home at the same time.
And the world will become more polluted, as it did yesterday.

Tomorrow's world doesn't look good.
The world's too polluted.
And it's got to the point if you want to go out you'd better wear a hood.

Chemicals are all over the place,
From vehicles and factories.
The game of survival is becoming a race.

It's not as if the matter is out of our hands,
We could use public transport
And start recycling cans.

Think of how life could be,
If we just put some effort in,
The world could be green.

We need more nature,
And far less waste,
Stop thinking of yourselves and become more mature.

If we're not careful, life will soon end,
Our descendants will not live,
But if we try, life will extend.

If we all work together,
We can make a go of it,
Make the world clean, *forever.*

Tom Ralph (14)
Borden Grammar School

THE TOMORROW PEOPLE

What is the day that will never arrive?
Who are the folk who can't see our skies?
When is the time when we maybe could hack,
into seeing their faces without them seeing back?

There's one special time, it's one in a million,
Something that's rare but not one in a billion.
The one tiny second in which they can be seen,
In their own little world covered with a screen.

This is where the future lies,
but not for us,
for those inside.
It's a scary thought to bring to mind,
That all is revealed then that chime chimes

This one tiny moment happens at New Year,
With the tick of the clock that strikes. Oh dear,
We blinked and missed the time,
When the tomorrow people would be visible to mine.

Ben Calder (15)
Borden Grammar School

THE DEMISE OF MANKIND

Houses that rely on the sun
To keep people warm and lights going on
Solar power, the power of the future.

People walking around on clouds
Living on the moon
Space travel, the travel of the future.

People dying from starvation
Deadly missiles fired from planes
Nuclear war, the war of the future.

Controversial food plantations
The only thing to keep humans alive
Genetic food, the food of the future.

Aliens invade and take Earth over
They tell us we are their slaves
Alien leaders, the leaders of the future.

600 and still accelerating
Breaking the sound barrier with ease
Supersonic cars, the cars of the future.

Pets that do all the housework
And don't mess on the carpet
Educated pets, the pets of the future.

The end of the human race is nigh.

Philip Hawkins (13)
Borden Grammar School

THE SEA

The sea is a lion
It moves with a crash and a roar
It leaps and bounds angrily
Seeking its prey
It ploughs forward
Lets out a wild shriek.

Holly Horton (13)
Clarendon House School

THE SEA

The sea is a galloping horse
Huge and white
With his great big hooves
And long white mane
The sea rumbles with the noise

Harri Stenning (13)
Clarendon House School

THE SEA

The sea is like a horse
Every day running the same course.
Throughout a storm galloping upon the shore,
Knocking on the sandy door.
And once it is calm, he is at peace,
Until it starts again, then he becomes the beast.

Jessica Turnbull (13)
Clarendon House School

THE SEA

The sea is like a prowling lioness
Pawing at the shore
Scraping her claws across the sand
Her body pushing at the land
She constantly pursues her helpless prey
And hides in the shadows when it runs away
But back she returns with the whispers of the grass
Her padding paws like the lap of the waves
And as she attacks she becomes fierce
Baring her teeth which so easily pierce
The skin of the antelope which silently stand
Like the statue-still cliffs and the golden sand
The lioness and the antelope are like sea and land
Always together but never hand in hand.

Emily Bath (13)
Clarendon House School

THE SEA

The sea is a ferocious tiger
Roaring and growling all day
Active and loud
Causing destruction and ruining lives
Brimming with anger
Eating away at the cliffs
But sometimes a playful kitten
Dancing on the shore
Chasing its tail
Darting in and out
Relaxed and peaceful
And lets out a purr of contentment.

Marie Brown (13)
Clarendon House School

THE SEA

The sea is an angry cat,
Blue and green,
Its big eyes look upon you,
It scratches the cliffs and the stones
It roars as loud as it can and puts up a fight,
Turning, twitching, wanting to get free.
Purring for help,
The sea is an angry cat.

Tasmin Field (13)
Clarendon House School

THE SEA

The sea is a mouse,
Running and rippling onto the sand,
On a hot summer evening,
Searching the beach for treasures to take away.
Snuffing quietly on the breeze,
Turning and twisting all the while.

Beverley Watling (13)
Clarendon House School

THE SEA IS . . .

The sea is a sleepy cat
It curls its tail around the rocks
It purrs again and again.
Its purr is so quiet that you can hardly hear it.
Its eyes are green with a hint of blue
It breathes softly as it sleeps.

Sarah Doyle (13)
Clarendon House School

THE SEA

The sea is a fierce lion,
giant and golden as the sun beams down.
He lazily rests on the beach all day and all night,
With his white teeth and giant mane,
hour upon hour he roars at the shore,
lapping the shingle with his rough tongue.
Through the day he bounds and leaps,
crashing against the cage he is in,
trying to erode the white walls.
As the sky grows grey, he rises
with a mighty *roar!*
He becomes wild and free.
Then as the night draws in and the stars shine,
he gently lies snoring,
up and down with his great chest when he breathes.

Gemma Young (13)
Clarendon House School

THE SEA

The sea is an elephant
Giant, and grey,
He charges up the beach
On stormy nights
Terrifying to behold.
He can be playful too,
Quiet and gentle
Ever moving, eternally pawing
At the shore.

Jo Johnson (13)
Clarendon House School

THE SEA

The sea is a beautiful ballet dancer,
Graceful and at peace,
Spinning, turning
Dancing and jumping
With elegant melodic movements.
She creates a never-ending dance
Then she bows before performing again.
Then with a flurry of feet
Dancers all join
They cause a rumble of waves
That crash to their death
They dance joyfully and pose proudly
The dancers make waves gallop to shore.
Then they scurry back to sea.
They fall graciously onto the seabed
Then they rise before the final crash
Then flow back to sea.
The grey cloud curtains are drawn
And the dance ends.

Leah O'Connor (13)
Clarendon House School

THE SEA

The sea is a cobra
Sliding gently upon the golden sand of the shore
Gracefully, quietly
An angry serpent turns into a storm
Arching its watery neck
And finally diving heartlessly upon its helpless victim.

Jenny Brown (13)
Clarendon House School

THE SEA

The sea is an Australian dingo,
Playing with the shore - running away
Over the Great Barrier Reef
And then back up the beach.
The sun shimmers like gold on his sleek body and shiny fur,
Making his wild eyes glint blue and green.
The dingo wags his tail, enjoying the game
And sends a shower of spray over the cliffs.
Barking in delight at the rainbows shimmering through
                                    the droplets of water,
He bounds back up the beach
To the top half of the shore,
Where he curls up for the night with his head on his paws.

In the night, the dingo feels uneasy,
Clouds obscure the moon, and the wind whistles down the cliffs.
The dingo rushes up and down the beach in panic,
His mouth foaming at the sides,
His eyes rolling.
Thunder crashes, and he leaps high into the air,
Throwing spray over the cliffs.
Lightning flashes and his voice joins the noise of the wind
Howling in terror.
It starts to rain, and the dingo seeks shelter under an
                                    overhanging rock.
After a while the rain eases, the thunder dies away and the
                                    lightning becomes less and less frequent.
The dingo feels at ease once again,
And peace reigns once more as he settles down to sleep,
As the tide quietly retreats down the beach.

Kirsty Barber (13)
Clarendon House School

THE SEA IS...

The sea is a raging bull,
That charges onto the shore devouring all in its path,
Crushing the sea life under its heavy hooves
And breathing odoriferous waves from its nostrils.
Retiring to gentle ripples and retreating to its enclosures with
The rise of the moon on the outgoing tide.
The water can lap up gently across the sand leaving the
Proud surrounding cliffs to erode and crumble away.
As the stars come out and the sun moves around us
He comes out to prowl.
His breath gets quicker and his pace wider.
Then, as the daylight returns to Earth
And the golden sand can be seen again
He settles down into peace and lazily dozes through the day.

Abigail Ballard (13)
Clarendon House School

THE SEA IS A...

The sea is a majestic beast,
It's proud because of its power,
But its temper is to be feared.
People are drawn to it because it provides food for them,
But God help anyone who is caught in its clutches when
It's in a ferocious mood.
The beast can be fun, playful and kind.
But can also be a wild, dangerous, cruel and unforgiving force.
It can be your best friend, and yet your worst enemy.

Christina Michael (13)
Clarendon House School

THE SEA

The sea is a graceful swan.
Glides, slips, slides
smoothly.
Then in a flurry of white
feathers,
it's gone.
Its neck draws back.
Beating silver-white wings
rhythmically.
The sound fills your ears,
Rushing, faster and faster.
Until in a majestic swoop,
It takes off and flies,
higher, higher,
Before landing.
White feathers flutter
down.
Then drifting out, once
more,
with head held high.
Graceful, serene and calm,
until the next take-off.

Victoria Moss (13)
Clarendon House School

TEARS ON THE LANDSCAPE

I stood scouring the mist,
My body adrift, it was never found,
To my left the wind and water hissed,
Along with the army of no sound.
Far beyond my right the enemy did stand,
As cold and as lonesome as an arctic cave,
They shrieked and wailed, that barbaric band,
I sold my soul to that demon wave.
Perhaps in the vile death that surrounded me, I saw light,
With those former glimmering shadows of almighty power,
Their eyes wept with what befell in their sight,
Although their hearts were shameless and sour.
Enigmatic souls radiated to the heavens,
As all sides felt sure of the others doom,
If only one man looked through my eyes at seven,
Seven the number of that creeping deathly gloom.
Powerless to extinguish the seething cauldrons of hate,
I saw and heard the trumpet players mourn,
As each of those seven armies rose to fight late,
Was I the first tear on the bloodied landscape torn?
Brave men fought a coward's war,
Never knowing if a sword sung out their eternal name,
The battle's law was simple; let there be no law,
And there was none.
I stood scouring the bloodied mist.

Robert Dickens (15)
Cranbrook School

TROY

Nothing in me. Nothing to break the siege of loneliness. No words.
Once words were release. Once words fell as
free as water. I blessed them. I was a poet. A woman of words. Words,
a sacred expression of my soul. The suffering I created was so real,
as real as the knife on my skin.
The scars are smaller than I imagined. Pale, the ache long gone now,
they are irrefutable.
I bled myself to try to make pain that would justify the loneliness. I was afraid,
oh God, so frightened, that I am a lie. A fake. No poet.
No person made complete, deserving, loved, *justified*.
I was afraid the knife would release the legacy of my birth.
That I was flawed, when I sought so desperately to be good.
I felt only my failure. My sin.

Why, if there is a God, is this all there is when I cannot sleep?
The fear. Obsessions chattering like fallen angels, raising hell.
Once I had words, even when I had nothing else.
Now I read those words which meant so much and they are empty.
I see only pretension. I see only cliché. I can't find my Muse.
She didn't come when I cried until I choked, she didn't come
when I tasted my own blood.
I write this and the fractured lines are catharsis, flawed as myself.
No more rhetoric. I no longer seek affirmation.
Poetry was a stage to flaunt words on, no more than a literary whore,
not the profound expression of existence. The things the past found
so searing are dead.

Prostituting the soul, parading privacy as art
I offer no answer, no beautiful words to camouflage
the hopelessly mundane.
Only consciousness meant honestly, tainted by shame
and flawed by inescapable lies. No hope of justifying myself
to a stranger.
Strangers, who can dismiss the words
and ravish the fallen woman, strangers who will never know
and need never understand.
Thus Cassandra raves, the madwoman, truth ignored as Troy burns.

Kirsten Morris (17)
Cranbrook School

KATE

She always had a bright smile on her face,
She made me happy when I felt down.
The weeping women are in dark black lace,
Everyone's weeping not smiling like clowns.

I feel so lonely in this hole of grief.
Everyone's weeping not smiling like Kate
A tear runs down my face like a dead leaf,
But she would want us dancing eating cake.

I will not forget my dear buzzing sis
I'll remember her fun, her smile, her love.
Yet having her around I know I'll miss,
When I am sad I will just look above.

As I grow old my memory stays true,
My lovely Kate I'll always think of you.

Thomas Malcolm (15)
Cranbrook School

MISSING

The emptiness of a room so full of things which were once alive
And will live forever in my heart.
The space, or lack thereof.

Like a prison with its bolt of steel,
Yet I have imprisoned myself here,
Away from all that is loud,
To think.

The guitar sitting silently, sleeping.
A pluck of the string for an echoing sound ringing in my ears and
                              reminding me I'm alone.

A glance around and over my shoulder,
To see the indents where the bed once was,
The bed that comforted him when he was home,
The dents that have left an impression on my heart.
The space.

He looks down upon me from his wooden frame,
So serious all tied up in blue.
It's like he's watching me, telling me not to worry.
His silken blue eyes fading from the sun.
I sit alone and silent.

Oh to hear that stumble, giggle and crash,
I have stayed up to hear so many a time,
Returned to the place where the young are divided from the old,
But for the neat folds of clothes.

He'll be back one day,
And music will fill the room like the air in my lungs.

I wonder which suits best,
To love a missing brother, or to miss a loving brother.

But I just sit,
Alone.

Gemma Reyte (17)
Cranbrook School

SOLITUDE

A room full of faces but no one to see,
A heaven of angels not comforting me,
A book full of pages which cannot be,
No one to aid me through this agony,

A world full of psychics who cannot read my mind,
Questions need answers which I have to find,
Beautiful colours so why am I blind?
Won't somebody be to me gentle and kind,

A cry for help which nobody hears,
Tortures and traumas I've borne through the years,
Frustration and torment caused so many tears,
Longing for someone to hold me near.

Louise Kirby (13)
Cranbrook School

FORGIVING BETRAYAL

When friends you knew to be eternity,
their love you thought was there for evermore.
But deep within a truth you cannot see
makes all escape through a now open door.

A candle flame can plunge the light to dark,
and with it take the light of happy times.
Sour sweetness, the two-faced lies leave a mark,
of friendship dead not worth a single dime.

Secrets behind backs are the worst attack,
to learn of rumours spread without consent.
You stop to think of gifts in life you lack
and blame yourself for lonely hours spent.

But we know every friend can make mistakes,
the ones you can forgive are not the fakes.

Camilla Hall (15)
Cranbrook School

'LECTRICITY

snap, crackle, pop
'cross the body shock
'lectricity is a slayer
frying my best CD player
current from the sky
setting fire to a tree
making my hair stand on end
yippee
burning blue, shining bright
keeps me up half the night.

Lee Whalen (16)
Cranbrook School

SAYING GOODBYE

Following the light as a
multitude of thoughts and emotions
soak through my veins.
It pushes and pulls me,
I reach to grab it but
it falls away.
I watch as it drifts slowly
through my fingers like
soft grains of sand.
I say goodbye to the light and
shining brightness of this star,
if it stayed any longer the
strength of it could have
increased beyond my resistance.
If it had been too intense
it would be harder to return
to the misty yet comforting darkness
that inevitably calls.
A light will come again
and it will be followed,
then I will watch while it
fades and I fall slowly back,
into the dark as I knew,
deep down I would.

Stephanie Whitelaw (16)
Cranbrook School

DREAMS...

'I slept and dreamed,
That life was some beauty,
However I woke,
And found life was a duty.'

If dreams came true,
Would life be that great?
After all not all dreams,
Provide content states

However the good ones,
Can outweigh the bad,
Sustaining a requirement,
To live dreams we've had

There are those dreams,
That stir up fuss,
From deep within,
Our consciousness

Then some so bizarre,
With the sense of a wall,
Leaving us to wake,
Feeling a fool

It's a befuddling matter,
No answer needs found,
For those many questions,
To this subject profound . . .

Rosie Donaldson (16)
Cranbrook School

WASTE

The tick of the clock
The rock of the chair
And the thin, grey hair
In perfect
Time goes back
And forth
To the rhythm of his flickering memory.

He is mindful of the time
As it passes away
To join the days at his desk
Or spent in all too infrequent play

What a waste of his days
He thinks as he wastes away
Nothing more to say
Or do even if he could.

He slumps to sleep at the
Dying of the light
And thinks what might have been
And could've been seen and lived

He tries to join his children
In a place so far away he could not say
Or pronounce the name.
They live in a different world
A whirl too fast for him to see
Or touch.

He never did too much

Francis Daly (16)
Cranbrook School

THE MATCH

The whistle blew, we were up for a fight,
The ball was struck strongly into their half,
It swirled and spiralled at such a great height,
Then down, down spinning into the mud bath.
Rugby players diving this way and that,
I came face to face with that big fat Matt,
He tackled me, I was completely stunned,
The scrums drove over and trod on my head.
I awoke to a foul clinical smell,
I was lying in a hospital bed,
My fellow players walked in, it was hell.
They were not hurt, but happy to have won,
They told me the score: twenty, twenty-one.

Ed Vaughan (15)
Cranbrook School

THE MONTHS OF THE YEAR

January's for snow and cold and a new year's beginning.
February's - for gloves and puffs and nature's springing.
March - is for Mother's Day and St Patrick's Day.
April's - for Easter Sunday and Easter Monday.
May - is for May Day and spring bank holiday.
June - starts to get warmer.
July's - summer.
August - is for autumn and a bank holiday.
September - unluckily is a new year at school.
October - is for a spooky Hallowe'en.
November's - for Bonfire Night and Remembrance Sunday.
December - December is for Christmas and the end of the year.

Olivia Nation (11)
Darrick Wood School

OUR WORLD OF POLLUTION

Our world is full of pollution but there is not another solution.
That we can stop pollution every day and night.
Every hour of the day I think pollution is here and unfortunately it's
here to stay.
Global warming pollution swarming, what can we do but pray.
Pray that pollution will die out for ever!
Carbon dioxide in the air good for trees, but not for us!
If only the world could stop and people think about what they're doing
and make a huge change to the
atmosphere.
I was thinking what really bugs me and the over all winner
must be pollution.
Pollution everywhere, it's a really big scare.
One day the world will stop, clocks will stop ticking, schools will stop
learning and nature will stop moving and then the world will
evaporate into dust.
But we can stop it happening if we stop travelling in cars, lorries,
motorbikes and get rid of factories
That will be the day!

Daniel Ordidge (11)
Darrick Wood School

THE FUTURE

In the future cars will fly,
buildings will be more than a mile high.
In the future we'll have two heads,
each complaining who has the bed.
In the future we'll meet space creatures,
all with their own wacky features.
In the future we'll live on the moon,
and use our minds to bend a spoon.

Luke Frizoni (11)
Darrick Wood School

Tomorrow

I have a vision, I have a dream
To see the world beautiful and clean.
To see the stars sparkling at night,
To see the sun shining bright.
I can see happiness, I can see fun,
People partying all night long!
Fireworks brighten up the sky,
All this fuss, but do you know why?
Because this certain time is special and rare,
It will come, then go and disappear into the air.
But we will always remember
What happened on the 31st night of December,
It is, of course, the millennium.

Adam Potter (11)
Darrick Wood School

Hedgehogs

'Hedgehogs are spiky and spiny.
Some are big, some are tiny.
Hedgehogs curl up in a ball,
Some are big, some are small.
A hedgehog said, 'I was nearly eaten by a foxy!
He said his name was Foxy Loxy!
So I curled up in a very tight ball,
I am not big, I am small.'
And the hedgehog said, 'I frightened Foxy Loxy away,
And goodbye everyone, and have a nice day!'
Hedgehogs are spiky and spiny.
This particular hedgehog was not big, it was tiny.'

Christine Wayne (11)
Darrick Wood School

CATS

Cats are cosy, cats are warm,
they sit on your lap and roll up
in a tight ball.
With their long whiskers,
their wet noses,
their fur, a warm coat.
When you are in bed
on a winter's night,
your cat is on the end curled up tight.
Black cats, white ones
tabby and gingers too, all different
shapes and sizes.
When you are alone,
you hear a purr and your cat
is there beside you.
Cats are companions who
keep you company.
When they hear the food tin rattle,
they run in and rub against your legs
with appreciation.
When you put the bowl down
they lick and eat with delight
and in the sun of a summer's day
perched on a wall not far away,
a cat looks over you
watching your every move.

Francesca Prudente (11)
Darrick Wood School

THE DAY OF EXCITEMENT

The first day arrives from morning to night.
The sunrise is burning like a fire in the sky.
I wake up with a fresh taste which brightens me up.
And I can smell the sweet scented flowers freshening me up.

Midday comes and the sun brightens up.
I see the sea, the waves lurking about.
And I feel cold and shrivelled up.
Curled up in a ball inside my small bedroom.

Four o'clock afternoon, I hear the sweet singing birds,
Hiding in the trees which are covered with leaves.
Soon the sunset arrives when the breeze blows against my face
With all my joy and happiness I will come back and do it again.

Rimona Barabhuiya (11)
Darrick Wood School

HORROR

Horror, horror, horror, he jumps out, Boo!
You think, what shall I do.
Your heart goes *boom, boom, boom!*
As you run from the terror.

Horror, horror, horror, he swipes your head.
Then you realise you are only in bed!
When you awake
You sweat like a hot cross bun.

Horror, horror, horror, as he pulls a sharp razor knife.
You fight for your life!
You than discover he is peeling your apple.
Horror, horror, horror, you're only in bed.

Nicholas Foster (12)
Darrick Wood School

ANIMALS

They come in all shapes and sizes,
textures and colours.
Could there be anything
that matches the wonder of these creatures?
Scales, spots, stripes and strength;
wings, tails, beaks and length.
Ecological miracles
adapted in all sorts of ways.
Some on land, some in the sea;
some in the sky, some in the trees.
But if we don't do something now
and just let the world sail by,
then now you see them
but soon you won't.

Stephen Tait (12)
Darrick Wood School

SWEETS

Yellow ones, pink ones, green ones too,
Brown ones, orange ones and also blue.
Toffee ones, cream ones and also mixed,
Small ones, fat ones they're all so nice,
But I think they're better with rice!
Popcorn, candyfloss and ice cream too,
Really they're not good for you!
Chocolate cakes, strawberry cakes, cream cakes too,
Lemon cakes, orange cakes they're all so yummy,
Especially for your tummy!

Lucy Hone (11)
Darrick Wood School

ONCE I HAD A DREAM

Once I had a dream
that didn't mean a thing.

I dreamed of a refreshing holiday
in the spring.

I dreamed of sand, sea and
sun and it had only just begun.

A nice looking hotel
where I could hang my clothes
and wash until I dropped.

Relaxing in the bath
until I popped.

And eat spaghetti with chips
until I exploded.

And all the computer games
had been downloaded.

Once I had a dream
that didn't mean a thing.

Natalie Bell (11)
Darrick Wood School

FOOD

These are some of my yummy foods,
Chocolate, yoghurt, cream and dips,
Doughnut, coconut, cake and chips.

These are some of my yucky foods,
Tomatoes, mushrooms and snails,
But most of all puppy-dog tails.

These are some of the juicy food,
Apples, melons, pears and peaches,
And any other fruit I can reach.

These are some of the dry foods,
Biscuits, flour, bread and rice,
Cakes and crisps are just as nice.
So there we go that's all about
yucky, yummy, juicy dry food.

Natalie Pennington (11)
Darrick Wood School

DOWNPOUR

In the cold, cold rain
You are lost but not forever.
The trees shake as the wind blows,
The rain hurls down,
Its only mission: to destroy the silence,
To find the secrets within,
To discover the locked world,
A place of thoughts and feelings
But it can't find the key.
Its mission has not been accomplished
And so it wanders off
To find the hidden depths,
Angry and determined
But it's all been in vain
The spell remains unbroken
And it rains harder
Trying to get rid of its anger,
Lashing out at everything in sight,
The rain will not cease its suffering
Until its rage is over.

Lucy Webb (12)
Darrick Wood School

MONSTERS

There're monsters everywhere,
There're monsters everywhere,
Between your toes,
They're up your nose,
There're monsters everywhere.

Be sure to be careful,
Be sure to be aware,
Because knowing the monsters,
They'll always be there.

Monsters are big,
Monsters are small,
Monsters do leap,
Monsters do crawl.

Keep your eyes peeled
Alive and awake,
You don't know what's around the corner,
Waiting in the lake

If you see a monster do not hang about,
It could be a wild buffalo
Or a raving trout.

There're monsters everywhere,
There're monsters everywhere,
Between your toes,
They're up your nose,
There're monsters everywhere.

Adam Law (11)
Darrick Wood School

MY HOUSEHOLD

Dad's watching rugby,
On the edge of his seat,
Not saying a word
Not even a bleat.

Mum's rushing round,
Doing all the work,
Washing, drying ironing Dad's shirts.

Sister and I
Our homework we do,
Help, we cry! We're getting in a stew.

Family life's hectic,
But never mind eh!
There's always tomorrow a brand new day.

Elizabeth Pennington (11)
Darrick Wood School

DICK TURPIN

D ick and his friends the Gregory Gang,
I n early England soon began,
C ursing, threatening, being nasty,
K icking, punching (a bit like karate)

T urpin moved far away,
U nder our noses, did not delay.
R uining things for us over here,
P unishing us, I tell you my dear.
I n the end we caught him at last,
N o one can be sure about the past.

Carly Maunsell (11)
Darrick Wood School

SCHOOLDAYS

Monday is the day
When nobody's about,
Rather stay at home
Than run outside and shout.
But it is Tuesday now
And there's no school so wow!
So Wednesday comes hooray!
Cos we all stop at home,
It's snowing, so no school today!
Thursday is here,
So do not fear,
We've got art, English, the lot,
These subjects are my favourite.
Friday is the last,
Of the school journey week
Come on go fast,
Cos tomorrow we've got off.

Cheralyn Humphrey (11)
Darrick Wood School

PERCY

Pink plump Percy
Lazing in his sty
Gazing up at the deep blue sky.
The farmer's wife dreams of pork pie
As she serves the slops of blueberry pie
Percy's ears prick up and his corkscrew tail flicks a fly
The pot-bellied pig lets out a sigh
As he trots over to his blueberry pie
Oh greedy pig, soon to die.

Roxanna Garnett (11)
Darrick Wood School

THE AVERAGE DAY OF ROY

Roy was a greedy and unattractive boy,
Any other boy or girl he was bound to annoy.
His trousers were bursting full of fat,
He took up the whole of the living room mat,
He smelt quite awful,
His hair was anything but delightful
And his teeth were quite frightful.
Every night when he came home from school,
He'd drop his bags straight in the hall,
Stuff his mouth full of chocs
And take off his most atrocious socks.
He'd put on the TV,
The smell of his socks now up to his knee.
'Good heavens!' he cried
Looked around the room and sighed,
He had not got the new X20
A Super Soaker called 'Infinity'.
He scrambled off the floor,
Stumbled out of the door
And headed straight to the shops.
With only a few choccie stops.
He bought this new invention
Making some man on his pension
Extremely wealthy.
And over healthy.
He walked back home then began to groan
He had no one to play with - he was alone.
So an average day of Roy
You see unlike any other boy,
Is as boring as reading a car magazine,
Or watching a repeated episode of Mr Bean!

Laurence Webb (11)
Darrick Wood School

My Mum

My mum goes to work and cuts hair,
My mum when I need her is always there,
She drives a little red car and
To me my mum is the best by far.
My mum is so nice, she doesn't moan but
What winds me up, she doesn't get off the phone,
She tells me things I don't already know and
To me my mum is always on the go,
My mum isn't boring at all,
In fact, my mum is rather cool,
She listens to what I have to say and
Helps me along my way,
My mum sometimes embarrasses me and
Quite often I make her tea,
My mum doesn't mind, when my radio is loud,
She sings along looking really proud,
Overall my mum is great and
I'm so lucky to have a mum like a mate.
My mum.

Lauren Brown (12)
Darrick Wood School

All Things

I'm entering a competition
but I can't think what to write.
I might just make up a little something
and say if it's alright.

The day is Wednesday, I've got a cold
and my teacher's telling me to get on.
'I can't,' I yell in my head.
'The bell has just gone.'

When I got home, I watched a film,
Watership Down I think
but near the end I got so tired
that I could hardly blink.

It's nearly nine I must go to bed
and think what to write.
And by tomorrow you can see if
you think that it's alright.

Ashley Pope (11)
Darrick Wood School

THE MILLENNIUM

The millennium is coming
Drawing up, close and near
73 days in fact
I can't believe it's almost here
But what is all the fuss about?
It's only another year.

It's only another year
Just like any other
Or, just maybe it will be a special year
For every sister, brother, father and mother
Let's hope it will be a special year
Not like any other.

Maybe we'll all have enough to eat
Maybe we'll live in peace
Maybe there will be an end to disease
Maybe all wars will cease
If I'm not imagining these, then
It's a very special year.

Katherine Marshall (11)
Darrick Wood School

I Wonder If I'll Dream

I snuggle down
in my nice warm bed.
A soft warm pillow
under my head.
I close my eyes
I think once more
I wonder if I'll have that dream . . .
that dream I had before.

Suddenly I'm in the sky
nestled down on the cloud up high.
The stars around me sparkle, delight
I'm happy up here with my friend . . .
My friend, the moonlight.

I float, I fly!
As I drift back to Earth.
I snuggle down
in my nice warm bed
a soft warm pillow
under my head. I wonder if I'll dream again
now I'm back in bed - at five-past ten!

Laura Stewart (11)
Darrick Wood School

Animals

I have always loved animals
And I think that you should too.
Rabbits, birds, cats and dogs
And animals from the zoo.

Some are cute and cuddly,
Some are big and round,
Some are endangered species
And are very rarely found.

Look for them in the sky
Then look for them on the ground,
Look for them in the sea
That's where they'll all be found.

Some are just plain ordinary,
Others are strange and odd
Some are brightly coloured
And all were made from God.

Samantha-Marie Harrington (11)
Darrick Wood School

School

I had to write a poem for school
So I said it should be cool,
I had a bit of trouble
Writing the word double,
So I started again
With a new pen
But then it was hard
So I wrote a card.
To my teacher saying I can't
And she said OK go away,
But then I worked with a friend
In the end
But we did have a fight,
But it turned out alright,
So we got an A
So I was very gay.

Ryan Nicholls (11)
Darrick Wood School

SCARES IN THE NIGHT

Lying in bed
in the middle of the night
I hear a bump,
it gives me a fright.
The dripping of the tap
drip, drop, drip, drop.
The ticking of the clock,
tick-tock, tick-tock.
It sounds like little people,
scurrying around under my bed,
sharpening their axes
trying to find my head.
I climb out of bed
go downstairs for a drink
Get a cup out of the cupboard,
walk over to the sink.
I look out of the window,
on to the frosty lawn,
into the moonlit sky.
It is nearly dawn.
A noise I hear behind me,
I turn around to see
a light that nearly blinds me.
I almost dropped my tea.
I scream and shout and it disappears,
never to be seen again.
After it had gone I heard
someone count to ten.
I was scared to my utter most,
then I realised it was a ghost.

Lauren Brett (11)
Darrick Wood School

BEING A CHILD

A walk in the woods
Bluebells what a sight
A walk on the beach
Seashells what a delight.

A long awaited trip to the zoo
Strange monkey and a kangaroo
A Saturday matinee
Wouldn't be the same any other day.

New shoes for school
Black or brown that's the rule
Pocket money you're to spend
Broken toys for Dad's to mend.

Natalie Gardiner (12)
Darrick Wood School

MY CAT

After weeks and weeks of begging
Came the joyful day
I went to choose my cat
From the RSPCA.

I did not want a posh cat
Pedigree or Siamese.
Just a normal cat
Special just for me.

Now I have my cat
Her marking's tortie and white
I feed her every day
And cuddle her at night.

Lizzie Ward (11)
Darrick Wood School

HALLOWE'EN

H allowe'en is about sweets and fun and scares
A nd there are ghosts, ghouls, witches and devils walking
                                        down the street.
L aughs of children running around and the sounds of
                            door bells and the cold wind howling.
L ots of sweets Caramels to Cadbury's, Chomp and Toffee.
O ctober the time is and lots of fun we have running
                            about up and down the streets.
W hen things jump out and scare you so much.
E veryone has fun and plays about and has excellent costumes.
E veryone has pumpkins with scary faces carved into
                            them with candles in them.
N othing can stop you from getting as many sweets as you can.

Scott Humphreys (11)
Darrick Wood School

LOVE

People make me feel happy
Friendships make me feel new
Animals make me feel good
Love makes me like you.

With happy and sad
Bouncy and bad
And things that are old and new
Like my gran, your gran, me and you.

When I am cheerful and sorrowful
Joyful and awful
Any way in which I feel
All I have to do is think of
Love.

Ruth Jones (11)
Darrick Wood School

MY SCHOOL DAY

I wake up in the morning getting set for school,
I got downstairs for breakfast feeling really cool,
I put my blazer on, followed by my bag,
I shot straight out the door forgetting about my keys
I met up with my friends feeling really pleased.
I made it to the woods feeling a bit weird,
It happened to be the fact I was really cold,
I came out of the woods warming up again,
I met up with my friends, chattering away again,
I finally get to school waiting for the bell
I get into my form room waiting for my teacher,
We start to read our books waiting for the bell.

As the day flies by I get a bit tired,
The bell finally goes whoopppeeee.
I get home for tea needing to do a wee
I finally get to bed ending my long day.

Matthew Adams (12)
Darrick Wood School

FISHY FRANTICS

One, two, three, four, five -
Once I caught a fish alive!
Six, seven, eight, nine, ten -
Then I let it go again!
Why did you let it go?
Because it bit my finger so,
Why did I lose my cool?
Because it was a shark, you fool!

Ben Turner (11)
Darrick Wood School

PRIDE

Through the darkness, good will ride
Fighting evil with pride at his side
Always call on good and pride
When you need a friend at your side.

Take no notice of the saying
Sticks and stones may break your bones
But words will never hurt me
It just isn't true but when evil tries to break you
using words
Call on pride to stand at your side and help you

God forms himself in many ways
God, love, peace and respect.
Model your actions into them
But don't be used by lies and tricks
Hold your head up high
Make hate live nigh
But if your world falls
Under the blade of evil
Your heart, good and pride and many more good souls
Will fight and tear through the dark
To victory for love.

Daniel Hoath (11)
Darrick Wood School

A New Planet

The sun is a flat yellow disk twirling around,
Mercury is a round ball which has a brown tone,
Venus is a sweltering lump of rock whose deadly
                               clouds cover the atmosphere.
Earth is a calm place to live but it might be hot in the future,
Mars is a sign of war from which the scarlet-red ball looks
                               like a mean eye of a poacher,
Jupiter is the largest of them all which can eat anything
                               and everything up,
Saturn with its glorious rings twirl round and round as it spins,
Uranus with its mystic green clouds go around and around in time,
Neptune with its raging dark spot, the smaller one speeds
                               round following its brother.
Pluto is the last and smallest of them all, it travels ever
                               so slowly round the sun.
Now we spot a new planet, could this be Planet X?

William Marsh (11)
Darrick Wood School

If I ...

If I was a millionaire, I'd spend it all today,
If I could fly so very high, I'd float and fly away,
If I was a submarine, I'd explore the coral reef,
If I could be a hedgehog, I would nest among the leaves,
If I was a fast sports car, I'd go so very fast,
If I sailed the entire world, I'd have gone so very far,
If I could find a sapphire, it would be so very blue,
If I wanted to have you now, I'd give these things to you.

Claire Lincoln (11)
Darrick Wood School

MY PAST

Day by day passes,
As I try and block from
My mind the past.
Forward I walk, but,
Following me it creeps up.
The future is my goal,
But overshadowing me
And towering above me,
Is my past.
For every step I take
Successfully,
My strong, powerful past,
Drags my weakened
Self back.
Looking ahead,
Is not possible.
My haunting past
Just will not let go.
My mind wanders
From a present action,
To my . . . past.
My mind immunised
Against my past,
Creates a barrier
Against it every time.
Defeatedly it fails.
Every day I awake,
Prepared,
For the continuous battle
Of my freedom,
To move forward
From my past.

Sonia Chana (14)
Dartford Grammar School For Girls

HOME SWEET HOME

Home,
The place I want to be.
Home, the place where I belong.
My home, my heaven.

The beautiful aroma,
of the Egyptian Musk
travels, from room to room.
The warm sweet smell of cookies,
Mother bakes, drifts into the
Living room and makes my stomach rumble.

Slow. Gentle. Light.
The Arabian music floats around,
Almost as if it is a feather.
The cats lie on the sofa,
Like trophies,
Placed carefully on a cabinet shelf.

The warmth of the red, roaring fire,
welcomes me onto the living room.
Tea, tomatoes, tuna,
laid out on the pine table.
Steam rises from the freshly baked bread,
as the butter melts, dripping slowly onto the plate.

My family's presence,
The laughter. The joy. The happiness.
Home, the place where we belong.
Our home, our heaven.

Nafisa Baba-Ahmed (14)
Dartford Grammar School For Girls

WHAT WILL HAPPEN IN THE FUTURE?

What will happen in the future?
Will it be like the past?
Maybe fierce brutal wars,
Or killings by the thousand,
Ideas become reality,
Like flying throughout space,
Is there really life out there
Or another galaxy.
Will time travel be possible?
Maybe cars that fly!
Every aeroplane will be like Concorde
And fly faster than sound.
How deep is the deepest ocean
What fish lurk there?
Are they bright and colourful
Or as gloomy as the waters they swim?
Will a computer be as powerful,
As a human brain?
Interactive robots could come of age.
What will happen to our world?
Who knows?

Kirsten King (12)
Gravesend Grammar School For Girls

FUTURE VOICES ALIENS

Aliens robots and other things
Will be talking among the kings
Of course, me and you will be no more
For we would be a terrible bore
If they were telling about spaceships and rockets
We'd be talking about holes in our pockets.

If we were flying across the sky
They would be flying by
In every single race
They would run the run, the fastest pace
They would win
And in the bin
We would go!

Holly McLean
Gravesend Grammar School For Girls

COCKROACHES HAVE LANDED!

Cockroaches ruling the Earth,
Don't make me laugh.
They can't be the new type of birth,
What a joke and a half.

They can't rule over us,
They don't even have any bucks.
I'd rather follow a bus,
Oh God, this really sucks.

Now, if they weren't so creepy
And looked at all like David Beckham.
I'd start to listen,
But I'd still smack 'em.

Anyway, that doesn't even matter,
The only cockroach I've known is my brother.
And if he tried to be too overpowered,
He'd get a slap from our mother.

Oneet Sandher (12)
Gravesend Grammar School For Girls

Maybe!

Have you ever wondered,
If every day objects,
You use all the time
Would come to life one day soon.

Perhaps the table would,
Play table tennis.
Or the books,
Might go to the bookies.

Chocolate will live on Mars,
Drinking glasses,
Will go to the opticians,
Maybe the pub!

Clocks would turn back time.
Computer mice,
Will eat crumbs and cakes,
Paintings will come to life!

Globes might suddenly,
Take over the world.
Rulers can rule,
That's what they do best.

But erasers will do the best,
Out of all these objects,
Erasers will erase,
Cruelty, poverty and famine.

Charlotte Irving (12)
Gravesend Grammar School For Girls

A Future Voice

When I see him walking down the road,
I start to cry, I don't know why,
Was it because I had some long lost feeling for him.
Did I know him? I had no clue.
Perhaps my parents loved him dearly,
I don't know why I'm crying, do you?
Who is he? What is his name?
Is this serious, or is this a game?
His face fine and delicate came nearer,
His face frowned his lips started talking,
I took his arm, we started walking.
His outrageous tales of a world far away.
Perhaps in a different galaxy,
He told me that the world would end, that the sun
                            would gobble up the planets
And spit them out again,
Rearranging the planets like stars in the sky,
I don't know why, but I already knew!
That night when I went to bed,
I had a dream about aliens, speaking a new English,
I seemed to know what they were saying.
'To all the adults out there and children playing,
We're sad to say, the world will end in 2360,'
'That's not fair!' said a little green pixie,
Then I woke up in 4530,
I crawled through sand and mud, but I wasn't dirty!
I must have survived the apocalypse,
As I was walking down an alley,
Again, I met that same boy
I started to cry, do you know why?

Lucy Fowler (12)
Gravesend Grammar School For Girls

What A Coincidence

Blimey! This baby's always wriggling, it won't keep still,
It'll probably be a dancer with no time to kill.
Justine's copying Lucy, who's doing her dance routine,
For her jazz show in a week's time she'll be a dancing queen.
Justine stay still! I need to do your hair,
Your ballet class is in five minutes, you need to be there.
Justine's really excited she's in the school play,
She has a main dancing part, but only found out today.
Justine has three A's, she's clever in the head,
She didn't pass her cooking exam but her theatre studies instead.
Justine's got the job; she's off to France tomorrow,
She's asking all her friends for some jazz shoes she can borrow.
Now Justine's in France and has a great career,
She's started playing an instrument but can only play by ear.

Emma Townsend (12)
Gravesend Grammar School For Girls

Future Voices

As we open the door onto the next millennium,
A new set of people arrive,
The young become the old,
With new ideas and new minds,
How will they speak out?
How will they live as a country?
What will happen to the old problems?
What will they think? How will they think?
These people are different,
Their minds evolve around the unexplainable things,
They live in harmony with only small issues affecting them,
No war, no disruption, no birth, no death.
Only a perfect world.

Suzannah Flynn (13)
Gravesend Grammar School For Girls

A WOMAN, WHO COULD CHANGE THE WORLD

As I walk along the stony path,
the pebbles crunching round my feet,
The light outside is blinding,
but in my head I'm dark as night.

My head is whirling with things to say,
About human rights, and how the
world can be a better place.

But then on the other hand, what's the point.
Who needs a little woman like me?
What could I do that could change the world.

Katie Smith (12)
Gravesend Grammar School For Girls

WITCHES OLD AND NEW

'Present, future and past,
Let our magic ever last.
Witches all reunite,
Guide us through each day and night.
With the power of the mind,
All secrets may we find.
Good or bad,
Happy or sad,
Give or take,
This world we make.'
The old witch chants
Now the witches turn starts.
Things may change as time goes by,
But traditions never die.

Paula Smith (13)
Gravesend Grammar School For Girls

BE WHAT YOU WANT

Unborn:

Why can't this little baby
stay oh so still and neat
Instead of moving around,
and kicking her feet?

1 year:

Oh Mum the baby kicked me,
I was singing a football song.
She is really sly with her feet
and I did nothing wrong.

5 years:

Give me back my football
you little squirt, it's not for girls.
You can't play with that you know,
you'll get muddy and ruin your curls.

12 years:

Every day at lunch and break,
you play football with the boys.
You should be with us girls,
playing Barbies and girlie toys.

18 years:

Why do you want to be a footballer,
it won't amount to a thing.
Why can't you be a Spice Girl,
all that money it would bring.

21 years:

As I run and score at Wembley,
those thoughts go through my head.
I followed my dream and so can you,
no matter what anyone said.

Louise Aldous (12)
Gravesend Grammar School For Girls

THE ANIMAL

Dark blue shards glimmer in front of my eyes,
Violet smudges,
Dust the edges.

Zebra swirls of ocean blue,
Mix with indigo light.

Perfectly shaped eyes,
Stare back at me without blinking,
Underneath a sea of royal blue.

Musty yellow fragments,
Outline . . .
A perfectly symmetrical shape.

A delicate black figure
Gently protrudes out of . . .
A vast array of colours.

Two thin sticks,
Dipped in a very dark black,
Sprout unexpectedly from the crown of . . .
A butterfly.

Rebecca Drewry (13)
Gravesend Grammar School For Girls

THE ELEMENTS

Earth, the home to nature,
Able to heal and to soothe,
Its moistness kissing your face,
Its dryness cradling you in its arms.
Shaking, splitting,
Destroying building after building,
Killing person after person,
Each crash a triumphant laugh.
Air, caressing your cheek,
Blowing the hair from your eyes,
Cooling your skin, refreshing you.
Whipping you, punishing you,
Hurling you to the ground.
A battle that you'll never win,
Just let the force complete its terrible destruction.
Water, splashing you, cleansing your skin,
Washing away your hatred,
Taking away every negative thought,
Until you are left pure.
Carelessly tossing you about,
Throwing you against the sand again and again,
Trying to destroy you with its powerful force,
Each splash marking a victory.
Fire, an unearthly burning goddess,
Both harmful, yet helpful,
Guiding strangers in the night,
Showing them a suitable way home.
Burning you, blistering you,
Its voice, the smoke, blinding you, killing you,
Filling your lungs with useless information.

Michelle Smith (12)
Gravesend Grammar School For Girls

SECOND WORLD MASSACRE REMEMBRANCE

Lying low, bombs all around.
People falling to the ground.
Shotgun fire, cannon blast,
You don't want to die first
But you don't want to be the last.
Soldiers running, leaving dead men in the past,
Running to the Union Jack flying at half-mast.

Rumbling tanks approach the hills.
Enemy soldiers make their kills.
Medics running to help those in pain,
Thinking the enemy are quite insane
To take all the lives of innocent men
Who just want to get back to their family den.

Blood and bodies stain the sand
I wish I was back in my home land.
Fighting a battle
Being slaughtered like cattle.
Onto the great death field we go
What to expect we do not know.

From lying in mud all covered in slime,
To looking at rocky hills we must climb.
On and on our bloodlust grows
Seeds of hope one man sows.
As soldiers, our souls we'll sell
To see our families safe and well.

After the war I joined the navy,
Meals of beef with thick old gravy.
But that's in the past my story's at an end,
My grandson's little truck I must mend.

Julia Marshall (12)
Gravesend Grammar School For Girls

VIDEO MESSAGE

It opened the door,
Stretching its arm,
It didn't touch the roof,
It didn't touch the floor.

It spoke in a manner,
You can't ignore,
It gave a warning,
It gave a chore.

It was from our future,
Sent by a girl,
It spoke in our language,
Put our minds in a whirl.

Its message was
To save a species
A species we love
The tiger, tiger when push comes to shove.

Poverty has struck,
And hit like a bomb,
People are dying,
We don't have that long.

Caroline Savin (12)
Gravesend Grammar School For Girls

FUTURE VOICES

The new year has come
It seems so fun.
To go out sledding
Even in the sun.

To go down hills
And through the village,
Past the church
But then there's a spillage.

Of Christmas cake
All over the road
I pick some up
Then find a code!

It's an alien message
Or so I've been told.

Could it come from outer space?
Or was it just the human race?

I do not know
I never will,
Perhaps it was a telephone bill?

Keely Underdown (12)
Gravesend Grammar School For Girls

THE SORCERER

Swiftly the boy ran through the woods,
Away from the blinding light,
Running, jumping, through the woods,
Running with all his might.

A perplexing sorcerer then danced round the boy.
Twirling, spinning and chanting, 'Ahoy'
Throwing sparkling dust on the head,
Of the boy he wished, soon to be dead.

Flames leapt up from every angle,
The ropes round the boy were in a tangle.
He screamed, screeched, shrieked and squealed
But still the sorcerer would not yield.

The sorcerer conjured magic spells,
And into the pot went three gold bells.
Some blood and a hair from the head of the boy
And the last ingredient (the worst of them all),
Went the screams and howls, and the pain of the boy.

Then all was silent,
Nothing heard,
All through the forest, nothing stirred.

Skye Fenton (12)
Gravesend Grammar School For Girls

THE TIME CAPSULE

Some children made a time capsule
Mathew, Lisa and Tim.
They dug a hole in the ground
And placed the capsule in.

A thousand years later
When nothing lives on the ground
Some Basle's land on the Earth
And start to scout around.

A Basle found the time capsule
And started to dig it up,
He pulled the box out of the ground
And brushed off all the muck.

Inside there was a letter
About all the things we own
Computers, bikes, brushes and combs,
Cars, books and mobile phones.

Humans were slow starters
Said an alien called Clout
'Their computers were very primitive,
No wonder they died out!'

Kayleigh Gilchrist (12)
Gravesend Grammar School For Girls

THE BEAUTIFUL ENVIRONMENT

The beautiful environment is a wonderful thing,
Birds, up high, to each other sing,
The flowers in their bed of grass and green leaves on a tree,
Outside is a lovely place to be!

But what would happen, have you ever stopped to think,
If we cut down all the trees and flowers, blue and pink?
What an ugly place the world would be then,
Everyone would feel sad and guilty, the children, women and men.

We breathe oxygen to live
And oxygen the plants do give,
The planets, not only, would disappear but the oxygen too,
So if we cut down the trees, we would vanish me and you.

Dream of a quiet sunny summer's day,
Where the bees are buzzing and cats do play,
The gorgeous outside must last forever more
Because all this beauty we must store.

Man was not given earth to destroy,
Or to play with it as if it were a toy,
If you cut down all the trees, instead of taking care of them,
You are ridding the earth of its greatest gem.

The earth is not yours to spoil, or interfere with nature,
Because who wants it? The people of the future.
They will look after it just as we should do now
So, to look after the earth we must vow.

This beautiful scene shows nature's hand,
Please don't make it a barren land,
So, look after the earth well, remember this rhyme,
It was not given to you by your parents, but loaned to you
By your children, for all time.

Sophie Cable (12)
Gravesend Grammar School For Girls

FOR ALL YOU BULLIES OUT THERE!

I want to tell you a story,
That could well relate to you.
It's about the bully and the bullied,
A story that could be true.

On the bleak and dismal Yorkshire Dales,
Stood a school at Monkton Moor.
In the school there was a girl,
Whose parents were terribly poor.

Her clothes came from the jumble sale,
Her shoes from the charity shop.
Gertrude Belcher, the school bully spat,
'She can't even afford a decent top!'

Miss Belcher was a mean, spiteful girl,
She hated anyone different.
Her own friends feared her,
For she was so intolerant.

One night when she was lying in bed,
She saw a bright light from outside.
Some little Martians were on the lawn,
Busily preoccupied.

She went downstairs cautiously,
And as she slowly neared,
They started to laugh and when she asked 'Why?'
'You're not green!' they sneered.

So the lesson Gertrude Belcher learnt,
Was, 'Judge people for who they are'.
So don't go picking on someone else,
Or little green men might come from afar.

Hannah Bishop (12)
Gravesend Grammar School For Girls

HOW DID YOU SPEND YOURS?

The countdown begins,
Every person is quiet,
The clock then strikes twelve,
Year 2000 is in.

Screaming, shouting
Laughing, crying
Singing, cheering
Kissing, hugging.

As the parties go on,
The night fades away,
Morning draws in,
Ready for the day.

Gossip round town,
Gossip round the country,
Gossip on the phones,
Of what you did last millennium.

Was it good
Was it bad
Was it cool
Was it sad
Was it daring
Was it devious

How was your millennium experience?

Katie Greenwood (12)
Gravesend Grammar School For Girls

LIFE ON THE OUTSIDE

Life outside these spongey walls
What is there to expect?
Voices of encouragement, death, no respect.

Once I'm in the outside world
What future is there for me?
I hope I'll make a difference to the new world
I'm about to see.
Maybe I'll be a popstar or a doctor curing ill,
Or maybe I'll be nothing, not even able
To pay a bill.
Life on the outside may be difficult
To the world I'm in right now,
So help me someone I'm desperate
Will you tell me how?

Life outside these spongey walls
What is there to expect?
Voices of encouragement, death, no respect.

Once I'm in the outside world
What kind of things will I see?
Happiness, destruction, hope, poverty?
Maybe I'll be an astronaut floating
High in space,
Or maybe I'll be an MP helping
The human race.
Life on the outside will be different
To the life that I now lead,
But I can make it, I know I can
There's hope for you and me.

Aimee Long (12)
Gravesend Grammar School For Girls

OLD ENGLISH ADVERTISEMENTS

The McDonald's advert has been around for ages,
You could even look them up in the Yellow Pages.
There's an old advert about the 'Shake 'n' Vac'
Their phrase is to 'bring the freshness back'
With 'Coco Pops' you'll win any race,
Eat it every day then you'll become *ace!*
Ambrosia Devon knows how they make it so creamy
The creamy rice pudding makes you feel all dreamy
'Nescafe' is about tea and coffee
Sit in front of the TV and stuff yourself with toffee
Chew 'Ice White' chewing gum every day
To help keep all the plaque away
'Dr Pepper' is a very fizzy drink
'Gulp gulp' I had no time to think
Argos, the catalogue, has lots of toys
Some for girls and some for boys
But I have come to the end of my poem and I hope you enjoyed reading it.

Sarah Payne (13)
Gravesend Grammar School For Girls

SECOND WORLD WAR MEMORIES

Lying low, bombs all around,
The injured falling down to the ground.
Cannon fire, bomb blast,
You're not dead yet but you may not be the last.
Step on a mine you lose your leg,
at the hospital there's no spare bed.
Germans coming at us fast,
The dead on the field are in the past.
Taking innocent men's lives,
leaving women helpless as their wives.
Hand grenades being thrown,
many soldiers thinking of home.
That's where many of them want to be,
not on the battlefield fighting the German army.
Muddy uniforms cling to bodies,
the dead being taken in army lorries.
Women working making planes,
there's no time for playing games.
Bits of debris falling fast,
the air raid siren sounds at last.
Widows and children broken-hearted,
into battle we were carted.
The war is over home again,
many of us a new life to begin.
Oh what a story we have to tell
those of us alive and well.

Rachel Willett (12)
Gravesend Grammar School For Girls

WHAT THE FUTURE HOLDS FOR ME

When I am born
who will I be?
Where will I go
and what will I see?

Will I hear
rattlesnakes rattle?
Or see a herd
of grazing cattle?

Will I echo the voices
that I hear?
Who will I go to
when I shed a tear?

Will I see a tiger
with stripy fur?
Will I hear
a young kitten purr?

I will have to wait
if I want to see
what the future
holds for me.

Sally Russell (12)
Gravesend Grammar School For Girls

FUTURE VOICES

'I keep hearing voices,'
I told my mum
'Now don't be silly
Don't be dumb'
'It's true, it's true, it's true' I said
'Now go upstairs and go to bed.'

I heard those voices again,
But this time I told my dad,
'Now don't be silly,
Don't be dumb.'
'Oh please believe me Dad it's true.'
'Now go to school you don't have a clue.'

I keep hearing voices when I'm in bed,
And this is what my teacher said
'Now don't be silly,
Don't be dumb,
Now stop telling fibs,
You're distracting the other kids.'

That night when I went to bed,
I heard the voice talking to me.
So I spoke to it back, I said
'Nobody will believe me
that I keep hearing voices.'
Then it said back to me,
'Well it can be our
little secret!'

Emma Drummond (12)
Gravesend Grammar School For Girls

WHEN I AM OLDER I WANT TO BE . . .

When I am older I want to be . . . a model . . .
I'll glide down the catwalk swinging my hips,
Blue on my eyelids and brown on my lips.
An audience cheering in front of me,
Wearing mini skirts and socks rolled to the knee.

When I am older I want to be . . . a teacher . . .
I think I'd do well at being the Head,
The school uniform colour would be red.
Children who are laughing, screeching, playing,
They're not listening to what I'm saying!

When I am older I want to be . . . a tennis player . . .
Vigorously hitting balls past the net,
Games being called off because it is wet.
One day my name is read out on the news,
What tennis racket will I have to choose?

When I am older I want to be . . . a doctor . . .
I will start learning about different bones,
Patients' voices, some crying, some moans.
Surgeries, hospitals, working in each,
Feeding ill people, bananas and peach.

When I am older, I want to be . . .
Well I'm not telling, just wait and see!

Johanna Nixon (12)
Gravesend Grammar School For Girls

THE FUTURE

I think about the future
And how my life would be
How boring the new lifestyle
Will be in 3003

There would be no one around
Robots taking over the world
No one needing to go out
No sight of boy or girl

The future is very plain to see
The future of us all
Green men with eight legs
Standing ten foot tall

People with three eyes
With hunched backs like hills
Trees standing like soldiers
Surrounded by unused windmills

My future fantasy
The future that I see
Brings a whole new meaning
To the words 'virtual reality'

I've come to a decision
A very bright conclusion
That living in 1999
Is the only solution.

Jennifer O'Brien (12)
Gravesend Grammar School For Girls

WHAT WILL THE FUTURE BE LIKE?

Will anybody have a dream like Martin Luther King?
What will the future be like?
Will we hear the scream of a toddler's young voice
Just when she's fallen off her bike?

Will we hear the cries of children being beaten?
What will the future be like?
Will we hear the yell of a wife and a mother
Shouting her husband's name *Mike?*

Will we still see the Ambrosia advert?
What will the future be like?
Will we still act out the plays from William Shakespeare?
Romeo and Juliet, Twelfth Night!

I wonder if we'll hear these things!
What will the future be like?
I guess I'll just have to wait and see!
But until tomorrow, 'sleep tight'!

Sophie Muckart (12)
Gravesend Grammar School For Girls

WHAT WILL I BE WHEN I GROW UP?

When I grow up, I'd like to be . . .
A super model, yeah that's me.
Short tight dresses and long slim legs,
With a figure that would turn their heads.

Or maybe even I could be . . .
The Prime Minister, ha, ha, they'd see.
I'd make the world a better place
And prance around in silk and lace.

But I think I'd rather be . . .
An astronaut, come fly with me.
I'd be the first to visit Mars
And drive in those galactic cars.

When I grow up I'd like to be . . .
Perhaps I'll just wait and see.

Jessica Dossena (13)
Gravesend Grammar School For Girls

THE BEACH

I was walking along the beach
When I found a crab's leg
lying next to a fish spine, it was fragile and brittle,
As I walked along, the waves washed up a dead, delicate jellyfish.
As I walked a little further I found a disintegrated mattress with gnaw marks on it,
Next to the mattress was a piece of jagged driftwood.

James Quinn (13)
Hartsdown Technology College

WAR POEM

Over the bodies I troop
With pain and suffering.
I feel like the way they look
My arm had disappeared
And yet I don't feel anything.
I drop in despair.
I want to go home.
This should all end
And we can all mend.
I should feel triumphant.
I suppose I do in a way.
I don't know what month it is anyway.
War, war, war, I'm sick of it
Is there anything else to do?
All such doom and gloom.

Vikki Spain-Gower (14)
Hartsdown Technology College

MY BEST FRIEND

Lauren is so funny and so brave
When you are down she's there for you
When you need a laugh she will make you happy
If you are down in the dumps
Lauren will bring you out again
Lauren has lovely green eyes
She has a lovely face
Lauren's hair flies in the wind, it is lovely
She is a very nice girl
Lauren is very trustworthy, she means everything she says.

Jake Tait (13)
Hartsdown Technology College

MY SAVIOUR POEM

The distant firing of machine guns
Broke the eerie silence
As I lay alone in the smelly pit
The rats crawled over my body
Nibbling at my wounded leg.

I cried out for help
But nobody came
I had been left to die
And dying I was.

I closed my eyes
I couldn't take the pain
Much more of this would drive me insane.
But then came my saviour
He was a stubby old chap
I'm not sure of his name, it may have been Jack.
But whoever it was
He saved my life.

Philip Shepherd (14)
Hartsdown Technology College

MY ENGLISH TEACHER

My English teacher is my friend.
All the good feelings she sends.
My class is as nice as pie,
To our kind teacher Mrs Alterskye.
The sun shines when she is near,
Have no fear Mrs Alterskye is here.
She helps me through my hard work too,
My class and I like the lovely Mrs Alterskye.

Danielle Moon (13)
Hartsdown Technology College

GOING OVER THE TOP

The loathsome stench of decaying flesh,
Many young and gallant men have perished.
But as the men waited to face their doom,
No fear was shown on their faces, but expressions of ecstasy.
They had been led like asses to a feeding trough.
They waited with bated breath, waited, waited,
Waited to live, waited to die.

Finally the whistle blew, and with a great squealing,
They charged over the top,
But many failed to negotiate the barbed wire.
Those who did were lost to an eerie silence.
The only sound was the hissing of the smoke
As it slowly crept across the plain.
Then there came the stuttering rapid fire of a machine gun.
The men tried to duck but in vain.

Neal Sullivan (14)
Hartsdown Technology College

SISTER IS BORN

It's June 25th
Mum's been pregnant for 9 months now
She should go into labour soon
Screaming comes from the living room
We rush my mum to hospital
Two hours later I have a little sister.

The smell of newborn babies as I enter the room
The only noise I could hear
Was my little sister crying
And the nurse's gentle footsteps.

Lydia Cassar (13)
Hartsdown Technology College

Woods

I'm deep in the woods
On my own
Exceedingly cold and chilly.

The stars are bright
My only light
The moon is covered with clouds.

The trees are spooky
Like mountainous monsters
Their branches are reaching out to get me.

The noises I hear are
Coming too near
They sound very hungry.

The roar of thunder
And the screeching of bats
Aren't all that enticing.

Nicola Woollon (12)
Hartsdown Technology College

Happy

Happy is the colour yellow,
It tastes like a birthday cake,
It smells like flowers,
It looks like a happy face,
It sounds like laughter,
It feels like a warm hot water bottle.

Hayley Setterfield (13)
Hartsdown Technology College

THE MILLENNIUM

One thousand years have gone,
and so begins my song.
So let's return to the day,
when William the Conqueror got his way.

Edward the Confessor,
his life was about to get a lot more messier.
He died one day on his bed,
and Harold yelled 'Hooray he is dead.'

William became angry,
and caned Harold with the help of Captain Mannering.
Harold with an arrow in his eye,
died with a heavy sigh.

Troubles came to the Holy Land,
and if you didn't do as you were told they cut off your hand.
So an army was led to go and fight,
and lots of men died but dead men don't bite.

Then people called the Pope an oaf,
even the knights who swore an oath.
And England broke away,
with Henry leading the way.

Henry was a mighty big fellow,
and if you disobeyed him he gave a bellow.
He hogged the food as well as the women,
and if he didn't like either prepare the killing.

Elizabeth took the throne with a smile,
and stayed there for a while.
Shakespeare played in his Globe,
and Drake, he sailed around the world.

Victoria was a powerful Queen,
and a lot of businessmen were really mean.
Twice we ran into hell and back,
and gave Hitler a mighty slap.

England won the World Cup,
honestly it must have been luck.
Diana died far from home,
and then we built the Millennium Dome!

One thousand years have gone,
and so I end my song.
So let's live the very day,
when somebody got their way.

Joshua Dunne (12)
Hartsdown Technology College

THUNDER

Slowly as the night goes by
Silver streaks light up the sky,
This way and that it clatters before,
As lightning shines upon the shore,
Rain comes down patter patter,
As the thundercloud clashes, clatter, clatter,
The storm rumbles
And bins tumble,
The noise is big and loud
As it passes the thundercloud,
Slowly as the storm dies down,
It leaves for another town,
Little noises far away
Will they come back another day?

Stacey Nicholls (11)
Hartsdown Technology College

DEATH SPEAKS

Boys ready to fight knocking on death's door,
Boom goes the gun of the cut-throat,
As urchins hit the floor.
'Run, run!' the officers cry,
As young men say their deathly goodbyes.
Back to the trenches the survivors go,
As hushed as it was but for the earthly groans.
All you see is skin and bone,
Flesh hanging from their plain faces,
With sad expressions,
They thought they were going places,
But now they are dead,
From the hell of war to a peaceful bed.

Charlotte Whiting (14)
Hartsdown Technology College

THE RAIN

I sit by the tree and it starts to rain
It is so cold and so quiet.
Where are the birds?
Where are the bees?
It seems so bare
It seems so clear.
The rain drops down and it sinks away.
Where has it gone?
Where does it go?
I love the rain
I love the wind.
Bye for now
I have to go.

Joanna Strickland (14)
Hartsdown Technology College

WAR POEM

There they sat, cold and tired
In the dirty trenches
With rats feeding on their friends
Petrified as they know they could die
                any second of any day
Knowing that they might not reach the next day.

This was no fun
Knowing that most probably they would not see
                their families again
Most of them were boys and were treated as men
They wished that they could be home
But that would only happen if war stopped
Many died for people today
If only today's people would respect their lives
And remember those who died for them.

Charlotte Oki (14)
Hartsdown Technology College

MY FUTURE

M y future is full of war
Y et people running free

F or their lives have no order,
U ntil someday one person will
T ell us how to keep the world in order
U s people will listen and put the world to rights,
R eady to
E nter our new lives.

Michael Hadley (12)
Hartsdown Technology College

THE FARM

As I come down the hill of the old track,
Towards the old rundown farmhouse,
In the distance I saw an old-looking pony
Standing taking in the view of the peaceful countryside.
As I took the track down
I saw an old chicken house covered in ivy.
It was like a carpet of ivy on the floor,
The birds sang in chorus all day long
And I could hear the crickets chirping
In the long hay-grass.
As I followed banks down the river,
I came to an old red-bricked bridge
Where I could hear the really light trickling water
That sounded really refreshing.
To me I wanted to stay forever.

Leon Else (14)
Hartsdown Technology College

MY POEM

I feel like I'm living in hell.
When everyone surrounds me
it's like a hungry pack of wolves.
Each takes its turn to have a bite.
The shouts and the laughter are like cannons being
released one after another.
I'm being bullied, I want it to stop.
Each day it's like being dragged down to the
bottom of the sea.
When I wake my head feels like a football being kicked around.
So what is the point of waking up?

Michael Carpenter (13)
Hartsdown Technology College

THE GARDEN

In the garden it was not very bright,
The time was autumn,
The leaves had fallen from the trees,
There was not a single flower.

But spring is coming,
The baby animals will be born,
The trees are growing their new buds,
And the flowers are starting to bloom.

It is getting warmer,
And summer is here,
Everything is bright and colourful,
But soon it will all be over for another year.

Hayley Wardle (13)
Hartsdown Technology College

THE SEVEN AGES OF TIM

Young baby crying for his dummy,
Little schoolboy wondering has he got the
right things in his packed lunch,
The young teen wondering about his health,
looks, hair and girls,
A young man going through university and
getting a degree,
An adult getting his true love's heart in
marriage,
A father retiring from his job and growing
grey hairs,
An old man getting ready for his telegram and
his grave.

Tim McArthur (12)
Hartsdown Technology College

MY FAMILY

My little brother is a brat,
He pushed me over on the mat,
I landed on my big fat cat,
She scratched my hand and that was that.

My sister is a big fat bear,
Her favourite fruit's a juicy pear,
She likes to push me off my chair,
Sometimes I think that life's not fair.

My step-dad Robin weighs a ton,
He said he wants to be a nun,
He really tries to be good fun,
I wish he'll go off on a run.

My mum called Nicky is all right,
She always kisses me goodnight,
Creepy spiders give her a fright,
She squashes them with all her might.

Charlotte White-Perkins (12)
Hartsdown Technology College

HAPPY HOLIDAY

Friends and family,
A new house,
Wagging dog,
Woodland walks,
Pub lunches,
Eating out,
Strawberry ice-cream,
Laughter,
Journey home.

Emma How (13)
Hartsdown Technology College

FROST

Slowly, silently the frost creeps,
People waking from dreamless sleeps,
Cars starting in the street
As people slip on concrete,
Dark and eerie is the sky,
But minutes and hours will go by,
The frost on the grass all crisp and white,
Like snow has fallen in the night,
Above the houses the sun does rear
Slowly the frost starts to disappear,
The sun climbs higher in the sky,
Brightening the faces of people walking by,
The sign that the day has almost passed
Is the frost reappearing on the grass.

Vicki Golds (11)
Hartsdown Technology College

THE BEACH

Splintered driftwood
An antique Somerfield trolley
A blackened firework
A smelly Nike trainer
An old sunken boat
Shiny worn shell
A moth-eaten mattress
A junk-filled box
A brittle cuttlefish bone
A bloodstained jumper.
These are what I found at the beach.

Paul Beechey (13)
Hartsdown Technology College

I Should Like To Paint

I should like to paint,
The wind as it rushes past me,
The electricity as it flows.
I should like to paint,
The rain as the droplets fall,
The thunder as it clatters,
I should like to paint,
The air as we breathe it in,
The hands of a clock whilst ticking.
I should like to paint,
The eyelashes of a human body,
The sound as I hear it pass me.
I should like to paint,
The heart of a catfish.
But most of all I should like to paint,
The world a different colour.

Kimberley Page (13)
Hartsdown Technology College

The Millennium

The millennium
is a very special time
for a family
get together, when we meet
long lost cousins or
new members of the fam'ly.
The millennium
is a once in a lifetime
chance. 'Miss it, miss out'
- as Live & Kicking would say.

The millennium
is a time to be happy,
joyful and kind, not
upset that your friends can't come
round. You only get
the one shot at this; unlike
most things in life, so
cherish it. You may find out
it's fun with just your
family and without friends.

Toni Sabourin (13)
Hartsdown Technology College

THE WAR

Men join up more and more,
Ready to fight in the war.
They say their goodbyes,
With tears in their eyes.
The first few days went quite well,
But after that it was like hell.
Walking through the squidgy mud,
All of a sudden we heard big thuds.
My heart was bleeding because of the fright,
To see people dying night after night.
I couldn't help myself from crying,
To see people lay there dying.
Most people passed away,
I really didn't want to stay.
But now the war has gone,
I can't believe it's been so long.

Carla Coates (14)
Hartsdown Technology College

Millennium

To some people the millennium is just
Another New Year's Eve.
But to me it is a lifetime's experience
That I will not forget till the end of my lifetime
And will always remember.

The banging of fireworks
The whistles and cheers
The Auld Lang Syne song being sung
By millions of people in this world and beyond.

Hugs and kisses are now being shared
By millions of people out of their chairs.
The parties go on to mark the night of a new era
And to welcome a jolly New Year.

Leanne Mitchell (12)
Hartsdown Technology College

I Love My Mum

I love my mum she's always there
I love her because she's my mum
She has some doubts about her
But has a lot of good in her
I love my mum she's the best
I love her because she's my mum
My mum is only 5ft 2 inches
And is a great cook, the best
I love my mum and her food
I love my mum because she's always there
I love my mum she's 33
I love her because she's my mum.

Michael Cooper (12)
Hartsdown Technology College

ON THE BEACH

I was walking along the beach today,
And saw the things people had thrown away,
A lump of raft, rough and soggy,
A piece of driftwood, grim and boggy,
A black and crusty baseball cap,
A dirty bit off a tap,
A Fosters can, rusty and old,
A Chinese doll, ugly and bald,
A Wizard tape, unused,
A Batman cape, all abused,
A Mars packet, faded and dull,
A tennis racket made in Hull,
A lump of metal blade,
A plastic petal the colour of jade,
A stone of a peach
All on Botany Beach.

Christopher Waddington (13)
Hartsdown Technology College

WAR POEM

It's 1917 and we are up to our necks in a fight.
Many men have been killed like savages,
Even our general has been killed.
So we now make our own plan of attack.
We are not scared, for if we die
We die for King and country.
If we clash with Germans
Our machine gunners would be put in to do their duty.

Aaron Rouse (14)
Hartsdown Technology College

BORIS

Boris is my hamster
He really is so sweet
He sleeps all day
Then plays all night
So nobody gets any sleep.

If only he would change his way
I know that would be good
I'd get him out and play with him
Just the way I should.

He climbs his wheel
Then whizzes round
He really does have fun
I love to watch his little games
My heart he sure has won.

Natalie Stott (14)
Hartsdown Technology College

LOVE

Love is dark red,
It tastes of sugar and sweets,
It smells of blooming flowers in a field,
Love looks like a cuddly cat,
It sounds like two lovebirds singing in harmony,
Love feels like silk.

Helen Lally (13)
Hartsdown Technology College

THE BEACH

The waves of the sea crashing amongst the rocks,
A mound of seaweed being moved as the sea
comes and goes,
The remains of a glass bottle smashed against the
rocks,
A shiny fifty pence, glistening in the sun,
A child's plastic spade left in scraps,
The remains of trolleys that had seen better days,
A deserted crab shell, lying in the sun,
The shadows of the cliffs make me go cold.
The sea cannot extend to the dry pieces of land,
A person's footprints indented in the sand
They disappear into the distance,
I wonder where they went,
I turn and walk back, just listening to the sea.

Louanna Coltham (13)
Hartsdown Technology College

MESSAGE IN A BOTTLE

Warm and wet,
Cracked and consumed by the salty sea,
The fragmented cork weakens from the
semi-shattered bottle,
The smeared writing spreads itself across the
teeming page like a fog on a humid day.

Danielle Cook (13)
Hartsdown Technology College

THE WAR WHICH SHOULDN'T HAVE STARTED

One week the boys are alive
The next they're slaughtered
If they knew it would be like this
They would have rather been bored at home
They're all getting killed like cattle.

Why have the generals used the same battle plan?
Why don't the generals change their plans?
Why don't the generals fight themselves?
Why do the generals want us all killed?
These are some of the questions we need to ask.

Sometimes I wonder how anyone will survive this war
Because everyone is dirty
Everyone has been bitten by bugs
Nearly everyone has lost their stuff
And nearly everyone is dead and gone.

Terry Lane (14)
Hartsdown Technology College

BULLY POEM

Sleep is my sanctuary from their constant taunting,
Slumber is my only place of safety.
The day begins with me dreading every step of the journey,
I know my persecutors await me,
Turn the other cheek they say, ignore them,
they'll go away,
But they stay; maybe I'll just fade away.

Hayley Jehle (13)
Hartsdown Technology College

SCHOOL

I stepped in through the iron gates, everything a child hates,
    Sloppy gruel like toxic waste
    Was dished up on our plates.
Aliens from another world hiding under skin,
    The teachers welcome children with a cunning grin.
Their plan has got to be really cruel
    I wish they'd stop serving gruel.
The worst thing is after school, everyone in the hall,
    The Head steps in, him with the big grin.
He's got the brains, he probably comes from the drains.
    Everyone says 'What is that pong?' As we sing the alien song.
The English teacher smiles and smirks,
    She looks around the class for berks,
    She'd pick them off one by one just for fun.
The cleaner is just as bad, he keeps kids in cleaning bags.
    We found out what he likes to munch,
    When we put a spider in his lunch.
He pulls the legs off one by one, he had only just begun!
    He would squeeze and squash it thin and flat
    Then store it in his hat!
Later on when all is still, he would have his midnight meal.
    Rats' legs, spiders, anything else
    He happened to find on his shelf.
You think that's bad, listen to this! It gives the other kids fits.
    No one comes out of the basement alive
    I think some survive.
I bet the cook has kids for tea, don't worry it would never be me.
    I know the dangers of the school
    Like the traps in the hall.
So take this as a warning friends, and listen to this advice,
    Never attend!

Douglas Sinclair (12)
Hartsdown Technology College

LOOKING ABOUT

As I sit in the trenches
I look at the pale bloody faces
    of my men
Who have been savaged by
    German monsters
As bullets are being fired
Men on both sides try to save
    themselves
As I see everything happening
I ask myself why?

Why did this happen?
Who started it?
It was like a nightmare
But it was happening for real
All the time I see men
    fighting for their lives
To save their country
When I sleep I dream of it
    ending
Every man reunited with
    their family.

Peace on earth to all men.

Laura Moore (14)
Hartsdown Technology College

APPEARANCES ARE DECEPTIVE

Some people think you're cute and sweet,
Soft and kind and gentle,
My friend, I know you're round the bend,
And marvellously mental!

When little things start to get you down
And your wings have all gone flappy
Don't scream and shout
Just go chill out
Don't worry and be flappy.

The early bird
Catches the first worm
Smile and you'll see
The leaves on the trees
The sun in the sky
And you'll be happy
Without having to try.

Hollie Marsh (13)
Hartsdown Technology College

BURGLAR

Like a cheetah hunting down food,
Like a vulture waiting for a kill,
Like a vampire sucking blood,
Like a fight waiting to begin,
Like a hamster trapped in a cage,
Like a mystery waiting to be solved,
Like a fish that hasn't been caught,
Like a hyena waiting to snatch a newborn calf,
Like a spider holding a fly hostage.

Tabitha Martin (13)
Hartsdown Technology College

The Storm

As the night goes by the lightning flashes,
Up in the sky the thundercloud clashes,
It makes a noise and a light,
During this boring, dull night,
It makes the garden glow like that,
It even lights the eyes of the cat,
The thunder is a pain to the ear,
It'll have to be the most horrible thing to hear,
The lightning's so bright,
It lights up the night,
The wind is howling hard,
It messes up the yard,
But wait, it is dying quickly by silently,
Now the night goes by lightly.

Alexandra Sabourin (12)
Hartsdown Technology College

The World's Fair

Poverty is a world-wide thing,
Thirst and hunger's all it will bring,
Illness, death and deep despair,
It's time to show the world we care.

I put the question is this fair,
To William Clinton and Tony Blair,
We look around at all our wealth,
Lucky that we have good health.

The Third World has money too,
But this is kept by just a few,
We could help to ease the pain,
Worldwide respect we would gain.

It would be cool if we could let,
the whole Third World off its debt,
Then in truth we could declare,
It's the year 2000 and the whole world's fair.

Hannah Skull (12)
Hartsdown Technology College

WHY I LOVE SUMMER

My summer holiday was really fun
I spent most of my time under the sun
Admiring the colours from the pretty flowers
that kept away the storm of showers
I sat in my garden near a tree
and often heard the buzz from a bee
I went to the beach and laid on the sand
I collected shells and got brilliantly tanned
I visited places I'd seen a long time ago
but saw different faces of people I didn't know
I spent some time with my good friends
because the fun we have never ends.
I had some adventures in the local park
some didn't end 'til it got dark
the weather was nearly always hot
this is why I love summer a lot.

Kayley Moore (14)
Hartsdown Technology College

I Should Like To Paint

I should like to paint a
newborn baby cry
Or the blood of a holy man
I should like to paint a
sea of souls
Or a happy family
I should like to paint the
sky of Mars
Or the River Styx
I should like to paint the
life of a new person
Or a new world
I should like to paint a
blossomed flower
Or a bright star
I should like to paint a
growing seed
Or a broken heart
I should like to paint
love
Or the thoughts of an
old man
Or I should like to paint a
brain at work
Or a baby's first thought.

Ben Catt (13)
Hartsdown Technology College

I Should Like To Paint

I should like to paint
a blue sky in the winter.

I should like to paint
the whirling whistling sound of the wind.

I should like to paint
a smile on a newborn baby's face.

I should like to paint
the relief after a war.

I should like to paint
the aches, pains, joys and pleasures of us
that keeps us all alive.

I should like to paint
a dying man's last thought.

I should like to paint
the happiness of opening a gift on a child's birthday.

I should like to paint
the freedom of all the extinct animals in the world.

I should like to paint
the exhaustion of an army man at war.

Most of all I should like to paint
a clean world with a nice atmosphere and no pollution.

Oliver Donohoe (12)
Hartsdown Technology College

I Should Like To Paint

I should like to paint,
Life in all its colours, its feeling
And the real colour inside everyone
I should like to paint,
All the colour in nature,
The colour in a plant or a tree
And the colour in every animal.
I should like to paint,
All the colour of the past, present and future
People saw the colour,
We see the colour,
People will see the colours.
I should like to paint
The anger in a tiger's eyes
When it loses a kill,
And the colour of happiness in parents eyes
When they see their new born baby.
I should like to paint
The wind as it drags a leaf high in the sky,
And the noise of the world.
I should like to paint
The stillness of the night
I should like to paint.

Elizabeth Kilbee (12)
Hartsdown Technology College

I Would Like To Paint

I would like to paint
the first cry of a baby
and the first smile
he brings.

I would like to paint
the atmosphere of Wembley Stadium
and the green turf growing.

I would like to paint
the noise of the blue sky
and the sun going down.

I would like to paint
the sound of the golden sand
running away from the
cold blue sea.

I would like to paint
the pain of a rose
when all the petals fall off.

Kieran Morris (12)
Hartsdown Technology College

FOG

Slowly, silently now the fog
Smothers the garden, hiding the dog,
I crept from the house
Gliding as silent as a mouse,
And got lost in the fog,
At large with the dog,
The fog was dark and grey,
It was like night, not day,
The shadows of the dark and gloomy trees
Made me tremble at the knees.
I thought I was lost in the fog of grey and gloom
thinking my life had met its doom,
Suddenly I started to see the light of day,
Then I knew the fog was moving away.

Stephen Stroud (11)
Hartsdown Technology College

THE TIGER

Runs like the speed of light,
Roars like a furnace,
It waits for its prey like a sniper ready
to fire,
Stalks as silently as a shadow,
Claws, as sharp as nails,
Teeth, as sharp as razors,
As camouflaged as a snow bear,
As snappy as a crocodile,
As strong as an ox,
Eyes shine like a cat in the dark.

Alan Dewsnap (12)
Hartsdown Technology College

PRIVATE WASLEY

The great war,
What am I fighting for?

There is mud and bodies over the floor,
I wish I wasn't here anymore.

I'm sitting in a trench all wet and muddy,
Sharing my last cigarette with my best buddy.

As I think about the white cliffs of Dover,
Oh I wish this war was over.

Suddenly the order comes,
Over the top to face the German guns.

I hope my friends don't see my crying,
I've just been shot and I think I'm dying.

Help save me!

Jason Wasley (14)
Hartsdown Technology College

HEAVEN

Heaven's like a funfair where all the rides are free,
The clouds turn into bumper cars and there's
a hot dog tree.
Everyone's floating around up there, wearing girlie
dresses and flowers in their hair,
God's in charge of parties and his Son gives
out the wine,
Where all the people can muck around and have a
splendid time.

Lucy Hughes (12)
Hartsdown Technology College

THE BIRD, THE BEAR AND THE HARE

At the back of my shed hid a mother bear
She watched and waited for the small dark hare.
Long dark claws, she sits by the door
And waits for a noise along the floor.
I hear a rustling, but it's only the trees
The noise is made by a whispering breeze.
Suddenly a bird bursts into song
And watches the hare hopping along.
The bear crouches, her fur stands on end
The bird watches the hare hop round the bend.
The hare keeps hopping, he doesn't care
He hasn't seen or heard the bear.
The bear licks her lips and stays still
She cleans her paws she's had her fill.

Tom Horn (12)
Hartsdown Technology College

I WOULD LIKE

I would like to catch the rays of the sun
at midnight,
I would like to touch the moon,
I would like to taste a flame,
I would like to see a tortoise run as fast as
Linford Christie,
I would like to paint a cloud,
I would like to hear a fish talk,
I would like to hear the sound of grass
when it's happy,
I would like to eat words,
I would like to see an elephant fly,
I would like to feel hot snow.

Cheryl Stace (13)
Hartsdown Technology College

THE OUTSIDER

I step out of my ship.
As I look around, I see confusion.
Why? I do not know.
These people are shouting and surrounding me.
With two arms and legs, they must be a rare species.
They also have a new language, one I have not heard before.
They are taking me away. Where? That is a mystery.
I am unheard of on this planet - so they think I am different.
I am worried. What will happen to me?
I am afraid. Anxious. What is my fate?
That I will probably never know.

Jefferson Regan (11)
Hayes School

OUTSIDER

You're fat, you're ugly not beautiful like me,
You're tiny, minute, as small as a pea.
But it's not what's on the outside that really matters,
Even though my clothes are in tatters.
Your hair's all greasy, not shiny like mine,
You're all bent over with a curvy spine.
But it's not what's on the outside, it's what's within,
Even though I've got huge spots on my skin.
You're on your own, you have no friends,
You'd be better off as a pig in a pen.
You know you like me, it's not a crime,
Making friends just takes time.

Laura Draper (12)
Hayes School

IT

Some days it's calm and watchful,
It's waiting,
It's wise,
It's ravenous for wisdom.
It's hungry for the truth
And it's glimmering, shining.
Other days it's crashing and wild,
Moving fast
Ripping and humming.
It's mad and angry,
It has no mercy.
On all days it's humungous, colossal and large.
It can be blue, yellow, green, grey and purple.
It's wider than anything else on earth,
Too big to see all at once.
It's *amazing*,
The sea.

Helen McCredie (11)
Hayes School

OUTSIDER

Outsider, Outsider,
That's what they call me
Outside, Outsider
That's what they say
It's been like this since I arrived one sunny day.

A Freak and a Geek
That's what they call me
A Freak and a Geek
That's what they say
It's been like this since that sunny day.

A lonely loner
That's what they call me
A lonely loner
That's what they say
It's been like this since that sunny day

Outsider, Outsider
that's what they call me
Outsider, Outsider
That's what they say
It's been like this since that sunny day.

David Simmons (11)
Hayes School

THE OUTSIDERS

At the edge of the playground,
The newcomers stare,
So lonely, so strange,
Just waiting over there.
Longing for someone to call their names,
A different lifestyle they must lead,
No friends, no nothing but each other,
How will they succeed?
Without any confidence to carry on,
And constantly being teased,
Bullied, questioned, picked on,
I don't know much,
But I watch,
At every break time I can see,
Those outsiders looking at everyone . . .
Including me!

Alex Wheatley (11)
Hayes School

OUTSIDER

Completely bewildered,
All on my own,
It's like I'm an alien,
Everyone dislikes.

It seems an invisible line,
Is separating me from others.
I look in the mirror,
And see a confused face,
All the strangest things,
That go on in my head.

I try to say and do the right things,
But what's the point?
I go to all that bother,
For them to give me grief in reply.

The other day outside school,
I saw their clothes,
They saw mine.
Their clothes were over-priced
Mine were from charity,
They stayed and had a good laugh
They turned back to torment me.

I hear the schoolgirls cry,
'Hey Alien.'
'Hey Freak.'
Nobody likes me
I'm an *outsider*

Katharine Christopher (11)
Hayes School

THE OUTSIDER

'Freak,'
That's what they call me.
'Loner,'
That's what they say.
'Geek or
Teacher's pet,'
I hear them,
They mumble under their breath.
'Playtime,'
They are the hunters
And I'm
The prey.

'Lunch,'
An empty table.
I'm surrounded by
Loneliness.

They tease me hurt me.
'Bullies.'
I run, I scamper until my breath
Is gone.
Then comes the pain.

So you, with all your friends,
Take a minute for me,
The outsider.

Martin Sharpe (11)
Hayes School

A Frail, Old Man

The year is 1948,
A detective's called to investigate,
On a murder of a frail, old man,
But the entire house was spick and span.

No gun, no knife not even some blood,
Just a frail, old man with a red rose bud,
He searched his pockets, he frisked his sleeves,
But the case was a mystery, that was easy to see.

They checked his health records, tried to tell his next of kin,
But he just lied there, the bloom at his chin,
He had no next of kin; he didn't have a spouse,
He wasn't very sociable; he never left his house.

His face was pale, as if he had been drugged,
A very uncommon way to die, he could have been
shot or mugged,
The rose looked suspicious, as if it was to blame,
It looked like it was guilty, with red cheeks of shame.

The detective gently pulled it from the frail, old man's grasp,
He plucked away its petals and gave a sudden gasp,
It revealed a capsule of liquid drug,
He inhaled some while smelling the rose, the mug.

The detective was rewarded, for quick and clever thinking,
The men and women clapped and cheered as the stars
began a-twinkling,
The case is closed, the problem's solved, the puzzle
has been figured,
The danger's gone, it's safe again ,the safety
button's been triggered.

Daniel Shears (12)
Hayes School

THE FAMILY OF DIFFERENCES

A long time ago there was a family,
but this was no ordinary family,
it was the family of differences.

Their daughter was as slow as a sloth,
their son was like a pig,
his wife was like a comedian
and her husband was like a dwarf.

They were like this as they were a
family of differences.

They called their daughter a sloth
as she was slow and lazy.
They called their son a pig
as he was fat, greedy and didn't
stop eating.
He called his wife a comedian as
she was mad, happy and cheerful.
She called her husband a dwarf as
he was short and stubby.

Their house was normal, their dog was normal,
the school the children went to was normal
and so was the rest of the family.
So why weren't they?

It's a mystery to some people and others
just take a wild guess.

Amy Pierce (12)
Hayes School

HALF-TERM

The time has come
for us to rest
and have a break
from doing our best.
We work very hard
while we are in school.
To grow up clever and
very tall.
So here's your homework
and knowledge to seek.
Goodbye, good luck and
have a good week.

Terry West (11)
Hayes School

MY BROTHER

                Screaming, running, crying loud
                Shouting, moaning, going wild
                Always getting his own way
                I never even get a say.

Nice, sensible, working in quiet
Sitting, reading without a riot
Always nice to other people
Even though he can be feeble

                Snoring, dribbling all over the place
                Falling, bleeding, always in a race
                Always being called cute
                I think he is an ugly brute.

Sobiya Yogeswaran (13)
Holy Trinity College

LITTLE JOHNNY

When Johnny was little he liked to play the fool,
His mother was over protective and his father liked to rule.
So when Johnny decided that enough was really enough,
He went upstairs and packed his bag then caught the 92 bus.

When his mother read the letter that Johnny had left for her,
She wobbled around, then fainted this caused a very big stir.
His father went bright red, the steam rushed out his ears
And when his mother came to she burst into tears.

Johnny never left an address but often waited to see,
His mother read out a letter for him on national TV.
Then one day his mother stopped and Johnny wondered why,
Had she forgotten about him, the thought made him cry.

So he rang once or twice, but no one answered the phone,
So he set out to find them but when he got to his home,
The windows were all boarded up, the place was gutted out,
He found out there had been a fire and his parents hadn't got out.

So when he laid some flowers in the cemetery,
He thought how it could have been different and of how selfish he
                                                                                  had been,
Johnny raised his eyes to heaven and in a final plea.
He said, 'God never let me forget them, because I know they never
                                                                                   forgot me.'

Caroline Mound (13)
Holy Trinity College

A SPECIAL FRIEND

I had a friend
No so long ago
But now he's gone
And I miss him so.

He was a dog called Brack
Whom I loved so much
He was always there
Ever since I was a baby
But now he's gone
And I miss so.

I remember every day
When I came home
I would get a big welcome
But now he's gone
And I miss him so.

Then that day came
When I had to say goodbye
I looked him in the eyes
For one last time
And saw not pain but love
An everlasting love.

Now he's gone
And I miss him so . . .

Leonie MacCann (13)
Holy Trinity College

Fish

The sea is where I would love to be
Under the sea is where I want to be
To touch the sand on my feet
Is really a nice treat.

All the colours of the fish are so bright
It does look very nice!
Hundreds of fish swim past my boat
Some fish pass and have a glance.

I wish that I was a fish
I really, really do wish
I would like to be an Angel fish
But I wouldn't mind being a squid.

I would swim and play all day
And pop my head up to say good day
I'd swim and swim with all my might
Until it was time to say goodnight.

I would explore ship wrecks with my friends
Play in the coral until the day ends
I would stay away from the sharks
Especially the seagulls and the larks.

And then my day would end
So I would say goodnight to my friends
Swim down to the bottom of the sea
Where my bed would of course be.

Nancy Sullivan (13)
Holy Trinity College

A Poem About Life

Experiencing life for the very first time,
A baby's loud cry or a chilling whine,
It's definitely a wonderful event,
A lovely gift that God has sent.

A baby's first sound and the pitiful crawl,
All actions are still very small.
When they stand up they fall down again,
Will they ever get stronger, when oh when?

As soon as they start to work things out,
They'll get up and walk about
And when they do they'll get upset,
Seeing people they've never met.

Gradually they will get quite a bit older,
With that getting so much bolder.
They'll do things that don't impress you
And things that will make you happy too.

From then on it will get easier,
Learning to cope with your fears,
Hoping that nothing dreadful will occur
Because they're freer than before.

Stephanie Aungier (13)
Holy Trinity College

MY PERFECT PLACE

My perfect place,
Is where horses run free,
In a hot sunny country,
The wildlife and me.

The sky is made of sapphires,
That will never fall down,
The ground is made of bright green glass,
That will never go brown.

Everyone is kind,
Wouldn't hurt a soul,
Like a loving mare,
Would care for her foal.

The clouds are made of cotton wool
And everyone can fly,
Like a bird
In the sky.

You can ride all day,
Over moor land and fields,
Galloping straight,
Stopping only for meals.

That's my perfect place.

Juliet Newth (13)
Holy Trinity College

EXCUSES! EXCUSES!

Sorry, Miss for I have forgotten my homework,
It isn't my fault at all,
It just happened to be today,
As I made my journey to school.

I was stopped by a man,
Who asked for directions,
But instead he put me in a bag for
No obvious reasons.

The next thing I knew,
I was bobbing up and down,
In a wooden boat a long way from town.

We drifted ashore
And at long last my journey ended,
Where this mean man left me stranded.

Now how was I going to survive?
If I hadn't made use of intelligent resources,
My homework, that is,
I had to use as James Bond forces!

I wrote on the back of it
And folded it in, DIY style,
To make a paper aeroplane, for it to fly across the Nile.

That is how I was rescued and brought to school,
Miss, why are you laughing?
Don't you believe my story at all?

Jade Simmonds (13)
Holy Trinity College

I'M TRYING TO WRITE A POEM . . .

I'm trying to write a poem, but I can't think what to write,
I'm sitting here in my bedroom thinking with all my might,
I will not leave this room till I've written something down,
If you think I'm giving up easily you must think I'm a clown.

It has just gone a quarter to three in the morning
And nothing seems to be dawning,
I'm just wondering why I can't write a poem,
But if something doesn't happen soon I'm going.

I've just written a line for this poem, it wasn't right so I crossed it out
And at this point in peaceful time all I want to do is scream and shout,
Trying to write this poem is just one big pain,
Before I finish this poem I will go insane.

May be this will be easier if I choose a theme,
How 'bout a boy who's never been seen,
No, that's way too hard,
May be I should just give up and be glad.

Wait a minute, I've got a poem in my head
And it's all about the colour red. . .
At last I've finished my masterpiece,
I'm glad this poem has come to cease.

Now that I look at poetry in another sort of way,
Poetry as beautiful as a summer's day,
Now I will say with a lot of zest,
Poetry is just the best!

Ekene Oboko (13)
Holy Trinity College

FRIENDSHIP

F riends are very special people
R emembering birthdays are special
I n good times and bad
E njoying fun and games together
N ever disapproving always loyal
D ependable, reliable that's what friendship is
S ecure in the knowledge that we care about each other
H appy times are our best, laughing and joking
I n good times and bad we're there for each other
P artners together in friendship.

Lydia Burocchi (13)
Holy Trinity College

LOVE!

Love is:
Love is gentle,
Love is kind,
Love takes you to places you can't find.

Feelings around hold you close,
Bad times good when you're needed the most.

Love holds you tight,
Won't ever let you go,
True love at least when you get it you'll know.

Don't let me down,
Don't tell me 'No,'
Because without your love, I just don't know.

I love you,
I always will,
For you and your love I would kill.

Charlotte Jacks (13)
Holy Trinity College

ME!

People try to change me
And tell me what to wear
How to do my make-up
And how to have my hair.

> That I need to change my attitude
> And take that look off my face
> That I need to get myself organised
> And take that look off my face.

Why people do this is
A mystery to me
As the way that I am now
Is the way I want to be.

> There's something they can't grasp
> And something they can't see
> That nobody can change who I am
> As I am who I am - I am *me!*

Sarah Mantle (14)
Holy Trinity College

War

The guns fire,
Lighting the dull night sky.
Morbid screams echo through the rubble
Filling the streets.
The troops march on,
Under cover of shells.
A continuous thud of their boots,
On the death ridden road.
The blood stained faces.
The water soaked uniforms.
The death.
How can this be justified?
Simple,
It can't.
They walk on,
In their eyes there is no end
To this blood shed,
That turns out to be their only friend.

Scott Tucker (14)
King's School

Trees

Trees are such wonderful things
With branches a bit like wings
Trees in the morning are used for birds to perch on
When they're perching they sing a beautiful song.

Trees stand firmly in the ground
Making not a sound
After 100 years they are still to be found
Trees, after they are cut down they make a fabulous mound.

The fabulous colours to be seen
Mostly green, but sometimes yellow and red
And when in winter they fall down make
A beautiful bed.

The roots are long
The birds make beautiful song
All these happen when the tree is young.

Edward Kevis (13)
King's School

NEFERATA - QUEEN OF THE UNDEAD

So many heroes tried!
So many lives wasted!
This evil queen, Queen of Darkness,
With her horde of undead rules.
The zombies stumble,
The wights mumble,
Once these were proud warriors,
Their souls corrupted,
Their eye sockets hollow,
Festering on fresh corpses,
They would have rested in peace, but the Necromancer,
That damned man,
Into unlife reanimated.
The shambling horde - Neferata's first ill dead
Rose to fight for their former side,
Soon to fall in the catastrophic cataclysm
To Neferata - Queen of the Undead.

Michael Labrou (13)
King's School

The Four Seasons

Winter is the season for most things to sleep,
a grey and white season,
time for reflection and the start of a new year.

Spring is the season for yellow and green,
when the earth awakens and new life begins,
a time full of promise and looking ahead.

Summer is the season when colour explodes,
blue sky full of sunshine from morning till late,
a time full of laughter and fun, a time to relax and enjoy the sun.

Autumn is the season of rich reds and browns,
leaves fall from the trees and cover the ground,
a time to prepare for the long winter months ahead.

Rebecca Fenton (13)
King's School

Soldier, Soldier

A fire of bullets
I fall
Tossed and shattered by the impact
I twisted down
On to a bed of pin-shaped grass
That bit into my wounds
Revealing to me a pain
Never have I experienced before
Yet I poured out blood
That like dripping tears
Made for me a soft cushioning
And an eternal rest.

Marvin Kissoon (13)
King's School

THE OGRE

The ogre, with its droozy mouth, (drooling)
With eyes so hungry, its skin so broumph (rough)
It dwells in a mursy, bubbling swamp, (murky)
That never stops frothing and burbling (bubbling)
Nothing comes near the ogre;
They wouldn't stand a chance.
The ogre with eyes so gimongous; (tremendous)
With legs as strong as long steel prands, (poles)
Chases them and never tires.
He captures them: they are so scared;
Their little whimses are inaudible (whimpers)
And when he devours them, every time
A tremengous roar rocks the land for miles around (huge)
Nobody knows why.
Scientists have longed to study this brenster, but with the risk (monster)
Of being devoured, they don't even try.
The ogre cannot speak: warblings are its language; (murmurs)
This bronst doesn't sleep, (monster)
It just stands in the swamp,
Feet loctill, like a guard at a palace (locked)
It primakes a faint drerbling noise; (makes; dribbling)
It's an evil souse, it has no allies, (creature)
Only enemies, but this foul vilety has no other ogres; (monster)
It's on its own, so lonely
With a fraley, it might be different, but still the ogre (friend)
Remains feet locked in the swamp, all alone.

Thomas Hourigan (13)
King's School

THE GALLOWS

It was a dull, damp, dark morning
As we heard the horses hooves clicking.
Pastries, bread and beer appeared
Bakers sold the pastries; innkeepers the beer.

Soldiers dismally patrolled the area.
Official officers stood high on the platform,
The gibbet stood tall and glum and
The rope's noose hung with impending gloom.

Suddenly, the crowd was completely silent as
The two blacked veiled murderers appeared.
The crowd motionlessly parted as drummers beat
                            with deathly regularity.
The men walked to the platform.

They stood on the stools
Mr Executioner placed the rough, hard loops around their necks.
Bang! They just hung . . .
Limply, lifelessly.

It was a fearful moment
I felt perspiration on my brow.
Wake up! Oh do wake up. Charlie
Oh! Thank God, it was a dream!

Charlie Beslee (14)
King's School

DREAMS

What is a dream?
Are they my thoughts and feelings of
What I need or greed for
Or is it a vision of tomorrow?

As I lie back, I think
What shall I dream?
Will I dream of playing rugby and score six tries
Or will I have a message that tomorrow I'll die?

Who or what controls my dreams?
Is it merely a game which the heavens play?
Is it cherubims and demons throwing my thoughts
Each way, each day?

What happens in a bad dream, suddenly
It is no longer happy and gay?
Why is it that nightmares never go away?
I lie there in a trance screaming
'Please just go away!'

I wake up sweating and panting
I say 'What a terrible nightmare'
I laugh and say 'What a terrible nightmare?'
I lie awake and say 'Just a dream . . . a dream.'

Edward Gutierrez (13)
King's School

A DREAM

The silence of the night,
Whispered in my ear,
The stillness of the air,
Shivering everywhere.

I hear the leaves' crispness,
Rustling in the trees,
I look around me
And all I see is the darkness of my imagination.

I had a feeling that I was not alone,
I looked around and 'Shhhwooh'
All of the birds flew out of the trees,
They were leading to a place unknown.

And suddenly I realised,
The silence of the night was not whispering in my ear.
The stillness of the air was not shivering everywhere,
I was not in this deep forest,
I was in bed, asleep, dreaming.

Jumana Abbas (13)
King's School

A Walk In The Darkness

Walking to nowhere,
Up a blind alley,
I feel alone so I look and stare,
It's dark and eerie, I mustn't dally.

My footsteps ring loud and clear,
If only they were quiet so no one would hear,
The echoes sound like horses hooves,
I wish I had worn rubber soled shoes.

Why does the road seem to never end?
I thought I saw someone around the next bend,
Shadows leap and dance about,
A dog is barking and somebody shouts.

It's taken just a few minutes,
But the walk has seemed liked hours,
I can see the welcoming light of home,
A few more steps and the darkness has lost its powers.

Scott Goatham (13)
King's School

MUD IN YOUR FACE

We are all lined up and raring to go,
With the pedals all set to spin.
The crack of the gun sends us on our way,
Everyone wants to win.

Slipping and sliding mud in your face
Getting in front is the key.
Jumping and dodging over the bumps,
You have to avoid that tree.

The roar from the crowd rings loud in your ears,
Feeling the cold on your face.
Tired and sore, shins battered and bruised
You've got to keep up with the pace.

The wear on the bike is beginning to tell
Suspension is starting to creak.
The front wheel is buckled the spokes are all bent
And the rider is weary and weak.

I must keep going the race is not won,
Only one river to cross.
The rider in front has just hit a bump
The line is all mine and his loss!

Stephen Slatter (13)
Langley Park School For Boys

BECKY'S DEATH

'What has happened to Becky, Graham?
Shouldn't she be home by now?
It's well past midnight Graham
And I'm forever wiping my brow!

There's still no sign of Becky, Graham!
Where on earth could she be?
She might have gone back to Gemma's house,
Let's phone her Graham and see.

I've phoned up Gemma and she wasn't there,
I'm searching my brain for clues,
It's been six days since we've seen her Graham
I'm giving up hope, aren't you?

The phone has started to ring Graham -
I'm scared it will be bad news!
A body's been found in a ditch Graham
And I'm afraid it's been abused!

Our beautiful daughter is dead, Graham
Why did it happen to her?
She didn't deserve to die, Graham,
Her life seems just a blur.'

Tom Reeve (13)
Langley Park School For Boys

THE HIGHBURY CROWD

The Highbury crowd roar,
The players enter the pitch,
The crowd are all proud of Arsenal,
Who'll win or lose one of which.

The Arsenal team kick-off,
From Bergkamp to Seaman,
They push forward with Overmars
Is he a speed demon?

Dennis Bergkamp is running through,
He is certain to score,
He plays it past the keeper,
He might score four.

It's now one - nil to the Arsenal,
They're playing like a dream,
If they try and keep it up,
They'll be a great team.

One minute left to the final whistle,
The whistle should be blown,
Their striker is playing really well
Great tackle from Keown!

The Arsenal team have won 1-0
They get their reward,
Just remember when the whistle went,
The Highbury crowd roared.

David Stevens (13)
Langley Park School For Boys

THE FOX HUNT

The sound of a trumpet rings the air,
The foxhounds are released -
They fan out into an adjacent field,
Hoping for a feast.

The fox by now is panic-stricken!
Fleeing for his life,
Through the undergrowth it staggers -
Fearing for its life.

On top of my horse I can see the pack,
Running like the wind -
I've trouble keeping up,
But always keeping down wind.

The tired fox scrambles on,
Sensing that the hounds are near
Passing the traps that are set,
Its mind full of fear.

The fox stumbles over a root,
Landing in a puddle of mud -
Shaking from head to toe,
The fox falls to the ground with a thud.

Here the tired fox lies,
Awaiting the final kill -
All is quiet around him now
Trumpets sound telling of the kill.

Mark Skinner (14)
Langley Park School For Boys

AXE ATTACKER

A man stands proud outside a pub.
His name is Stalker Jack.
His eyes can nearly sense the blood,
He holds behind an axe!

That monster waiting for his prey
And coldly he does stand.
Why here again, he lifts his arm
His weapon in his hand.

He's five foot seven and built to kill,
With light brown spiky hair.
In jeans and jacket and big black boots,
He gives an evil stare.

One chop he makes and screams are heard,
But did not kill that day.
His prey fought back with all his might.
Max turned and ran away.

The Police want help most urgently,
To catch the evil Max.
Before he kills a passer-by,
Wielding his dreaded axe.

Robbie Houghton (13)
Langley Park School For Boys

MY SISTER LEAVES HOME FOR UNI

My sister left for Manchester
About two weeks ago,
We packed the car with all her stuff
And she left the house with Jo.

When we finally got there
We unpacked all the stuff,
We stayed for a bit then said goodbye
And she tried to keep tough.

We came back home feeling sad
And turned the TV on.
We got a bit over our sister's loss,
But something still was wrong.

When we walk into her room
We realise she is gone,
But she'll come back at Christmastime -
It shan't be too long.

I love my sister lots and lots -
She is the lightning.
When she comes back home at Christmas
We will all be fighting.

Peter Stylianou (14)
Langley Park School For Boys

AVALANCHE

Despite the avalanche warnings
Of not to ski the slopes,
What was a fun adventure
Became a day with no hope.

The noises came from up above
Killed skies one by one.
A young girl, age 26,
Her life was almost done.

The sheets of snow came crashing down,
She tried to ski away,
The avalanche caught her up,
She never lived another day.

The boyfriend tried to dig her out
Only using his bare hands.
The rescuers started to help
As the helicopter land.

They laid her on a stretcher
And hoisted her over head,
But on the way to the hospital,
It was announced 'She's dead!'

Richard Mitchell (13)
Langley Park School For Boys

BUS JOYRIDER

Around five o'clock in the morning
A disturbing noise is heard,
A rogue driver is on the loose
Heading for Chislehurst.

He starts in Catford bus garage
Its number is 124,
Now a madman is on the streets
And is breaking the law.

Soon he's in a petrol station
And reverses into a glass door.
Now he's finally smashed something
And is screaming out for more.

As cables dangle in mid-air
The rear window has gone
And as the driver speeds away
A huge police chase is on.

Now the sounds of sirens are heard,
The driver can't relax.
Instead of this the police could be
Hunting a man with an axe.

Despite all this he keeps on driving
But suddenly grinds to a halt!
He thinks to himself for a split second
That hijacking's not his sort.

Eventually he stops the bus
And legs it far away.
He dumped the bus in Ashfield Lane
And wasn't seen that day!

Samuel Fox (13)
Langley Park School For Boys

Christmas

Christmas is a happy time of year.
When all dads drink loads of beer.
Children are so happy to see their presents
And one of them is a train.
When mum says dinner is on the table.
Then they act like horses in the stable.
They all danced around the tree outside
In the middle of the snow storm.
They danced and sang Christmas songs around the tree before
Dinner at dawn in the middle of the snow storm.
There was loads to eat.
Some were spicy and some were sweet.
There was a cake with a chocolate flake.
The crackers went bang and everybody sang.
They ate and ate but did not give their tummies a break.
Mum made a cake but then afterwards she said
'Cor I need a break.'
Because she made a mistake with the cake.

Jennifer Hicks (13)
Marjorie McClure Special School

In The Boat

The boat moves up and down on the waves.
The boat leaves the port in the park,
The boat goes through the middle of the sailing boats.
Down the river goes the boat past the houses.
Where are the lifejackets?
The boats come in the harbour the other way.
The river is coming all the way to the lake.
The lake is going all the way round the park.

Mark Cayzer (12)
Marjorie McClure Special School

ALL ABOUT MY DOGS

My dogs are nice and cuddly
And they've got waggly tails
And they are soft
And it's a black Labrador
It sleeps on the settee
And when she's naughty
She puts her tail down
And looks sad
And my sheep dog is soft
Cuddly and playful
And sleeps on my bed
And she pinches shoes and slippers
And she digs up the garden.
They sit and watch me go in a taxi,
To school in the morning
They wait till I get home
When I get home they jump up at me.
Then they go and get a toy
And wait for me to go in the garden.

Laura Buxton (13)
Marjorie McClure Special School

I HAD NO FRIENDS AT ALL

I had no friends at all until you came my way
And now we play and play all day.
I only hope you never have to go away.
It would be sad to lose the only friend I've
Ever had.

Caraline Thompson (11)
Marjorie McClure Special School

HAMSTER

We got Snoopy, the hamster at the pet shop
She has a big case
And a little house
When we call her name
She pokes out her face
Out she comes
She sniffs around the floor
And sits upon the bean bag
We have to chase her sometimes
Because she likes to chew
The wires of the TV
Because it's not good to do
And she likes toast and apples.

Michael Waters (12)
Marjorie McClure Special School

PE

I like PE
Games
Dancing
On the run

Bouncing balls
Shouting, sorry! Bump! Crash!
Whistle, stop quiet

Pleased to win
Boo! To lose
Quickly as you can
Getting ready, shirts and shorts.

Matthew Brockhouse (12)
Marjorie McClure Special School

TOM MY CAT

Tom is a tabby cat
We got her from the pet shop
We got a ball and a basket
Cat biscuits, meat, water and milk.

Licks your hand
Going slowly, going fast
Chases my hand
Rolls over gentle paws.

Charli Wheeler (11)
Marjorie McClure Special School

A NEW YEAR

The last piece of snow melts
The sun rises up above the horizon
Fireworks shoot up into the air and produce
                    a shower of sparkling light
People party in the streets
To welcome the New Year.

Leaves drift through the air
Birds sing softly in their nests
The year changes to new figures
As the church clock sounds twelve
To welcome the New Year.

Drinks clash into each other
Junk food lies on paper plates
Whistles, party hats held by happy hands
As the television announces the news and
To welcome the New Year.

Sarah Broadbent (11)
Newstead Wood School

CIRCLES

The full moon out at night,
Huge staring eyes to give you a fright.
The sun is shining out with glee
And the clock ticking the time for me.

The lid of a jar,
The wheel of a car.
A teddy bear's nose
And a knob on a door that you close.

The centre of a flower that gives out a lovely smell,
A ring on your finger to look pretty as well.
The top of a drawing pin, pinned in the wall
And a miniature multicoloured ball.

Zoe Tovell (11)
Newstead Wood School

RUN, RUN, RUN.

Shouting, screaming,
People disappearing,
Babies crying,
People trying,
Shouts of pain,
It's war again!
Fierce looks of anger,
War paint,
Hide before it's too late.
Grab your weapon,
What's going to happen?
Run, run, run.

Laura Brown (11)
Newstead Wood School

KING OF THE RIVERS

Swimming gracefully in the water,
Diving for fish,
Sits alert on the bank eating,
Suddenly it sits up
And with a flick of its tail and a splash it's gone.
Its clear, flute like whistle pierces the night air,
Its brown, slim body cuts the water.
The only traces of it are small footprints or fish bones,
But the ferns are still moving by the river,
Betraying the fact it was there.
A creamy white stomach,
A brown, furry back,
Brown, melting eyes,
Little, brown ears.
It plays with stones,
It's like a child in its play,
While talent is spent on hunting.
While on a diet of three fish a day,
It smuggles another two down.
Its pace is fast,
Its mind quick.
With only its back showing it looks like a log,
It thinks of salmon, minnow and trout.
It's alert,
It's powerful,
It's graceful,
It's mighty.
Prince of the streams,
King of the rivers,
The otter.

Eleanor Swift (11)
Newstead Wood School

SNOWFALL

The snow muffles all sound as more snow falls
The stars are frozen, lonely in the sky.
Nothing moves as the night grows and time crawls
The world believes that life has passed it by,
The trees move as a noiseless cold wind blows.
Uncertainty lies heavy on the air:
Is this the end, when everything goes?
No light, no life, no sound, no one to care,
The darkness of the earth, its silent plight
The sky is black, the creeping shadows grey;
A treetop, bathed in an unearthly light,
It shines, then fades - a star, dying away.
The silence makes an atmosphere of doom -
Eternal night, and everlasting gloom.

Kit Hopkin (12)
Newstead Wood School

MISSING YOU

I stand alone on the street corner.
The wind whips through my hair
As I close my eyes, and just for a second,
Try to imagine you're there.

I can almost hear your gentle voice
Whisper in my ear,
As raindrops trickle down my cheeks,
Mimicking my tears.

The deep voice of thunder laughs at me,
Mocking my sobbing heart,
Who cries at the memory of the life I lost
When our souls were torn apart.

The wind howls for years gone by,
For the love we had before.
I long for the day when I'll see you again
And I will cry no more.

Saskia Stevenson (14)
Newstead Wood School

SPORT

Sport is all huff and puff,
Aching and breathless,
That sort of stuff.

Why is there always strain?
There's soreness and suffering,
Behind the gain.

Hockey, netball, golf and bowls,
Endless frustration,
Before the goals.

The heart, the lung, they're all on strike,
Perspiration,
My skin doesn't like.

All the children have slim features,
But bulging with muscles,
I'm the games teacher!

Kirsty Brett (11)
Newstead Wood School

SPARE A THOUGHT

I hear the harsh clattering of rain on the ground,
But I see no crowds rushing under umbrellas,
Or pavements glistening with muddy puddles.
I feel the pain of small, sharp objects hitting my face,
But I see no gang of laughing children, throwing stones.
I smell the warm, delicious scent of food,
But I cannot see the way that leads to it,
Spare a thought for a poor blind man.

I fix my eyes on my school books
Try to ignore the other children,
Taunting, comparing our faces.
I cower, confused, in the corner of the playground
As bruises appear on my body, heart and mind.
I compare the differences between them and me,
Them and me, or them against me,
Spare a thought for a victim of racist abuse.

I drag my bare feet along the dusty earth track,
My toes are cut and sore from the stones,
A simple clay pot is on my head,
I lay awake at night, as my mother cries with fever.
But there is no food or water to give to her,
Nor a doctor to help.
I tear my shirt on a dry, dead branch,
My father beats me,
For I have no other clothes,
Spare a thought for an African child living in poverty,
Please spare a thought.

Sarah Burnett (12)
Newstead Wood School

DOZING IN THE GROUNDS OF AN OXFORD COLLEGE

With head leaning on a rough stone wall
And legs sprawled out beneath me,
My eyes glare ahead -
Tainted by constant shouts in peculiar foreign tongues -
(mainly Japanese methinks) -
My mind tires of the omnipresent scuffing of sneakers over
The stony surroundings.
As my eyes close and my ignorant mind is plunged into
A dim darkness,
Still my ears cling to the sonorous clang of midday.
As bicycle-wielding bow-tie-sporting slacks-and-jacketed men appear,
People scurry like mice to their lectures and seminars,
Their liars and lovers,
Their innermost thoughts - their unique lives,
Yet all I do is doze;
I doze and I hope -
And that's all I do.

H B Bryant (16)
Newstead Wood School

BABY

Alone,
Trapped,
Wrapped away in its own little world,
Helpless,
Curled up in a blanket of life.

Clare Lambourne (11)
Newstead Wood School

THE ORIGAMI FIASCO

I knew you were coming
so I built a boat for the occasion
as I always did,
only this one was
the most magnificent of them all,
the very best and strongest
of all amateur origami.

Even before I saw you
I launched my beloved vessel
on her Maiden Voyage;
assumed a safe and successful crossing.

You came and made the first ripples,
blew the first breath of wind
that sent her off course,
but she was strong
and overcame the storm.
Then you guided my clumsy fingers
to the water, let me stir it,
made me believe I could do no harm
and watched her founder
on the cruel waves.

You led me away as her white hull
met murky depths,
saying goodbye to my world,
and plunged into yours.

Stephanie Matthews (17)
Newstead Wood School

OUTSIDE THE WINDOW

Outside my bedroom window
It is raining
It seems still out there like
A drawn portrait by an artist.
The only movements of life I
Can see are the trees swaying
In the howling wind and a
Solitary bird flying across the sky.
The only sound I can hear is
My contented cat George
Purring deeply in my ear.
Sometimes the muffled hum of a
Car hurtling past disturbs my thoughts.
In my back garden I can see lofty
Crooked trees, bushy plants and
Luscious grass, a more vivid green
Than the emerald in my ring.
George trots off, it is silent again except
For the siren of an ambulance
Whirring past.
It seems very late but it is only around
Half past four in the afternoon.
I glance up at the sky, it is dull
Grey like a smudged pencil across
A sheet of white paper.
I look far beyond, I pick out some
Buildings lit up in startling colours,
Everything is still
And silent again.

Stacey Martin (12)
Rainham Mark Grammar School

HELP!

Help! They cry
Why?
No food, no water,
Help us to survive!

Help! They cry
Diseases creeping up on them
No seeds to grow food in,
Nothing.

Help! They cry
Their skin sweating in the hot sun
Why?
Please help or soon they will die.

Sonia Sharma (11)
Rainham School For Girls

CHILDREN TO HELP

All those poor children,
With no money,
No food,
No drink,
Having to walk a mile for water every day,
You've got to do something,
You've just got to,
So send some money,
To those in need,
Or send some money to the NSPCC.

Faye Pinkney (11)
Rainham School For Girls

CHILDREN!

Children, children,
All around the world,
Sleeping in boxes small, round and curled.

They beg for food or your money,
It's a serious matter!
So don't think it's funny!

There are a lot of children,
Who have runaway,
Now they're ready to face a new day.

Only they know what it's like,
To starve every day and night!

Sharon Wills (12)
Rainham School For Girls

TWINS

You are me,
And I'm you,
We are one,
As you are two.

We the same,
But are two in the mirror,
The connection between us,
Is nothing short of amazing.

There's a strong bond,
You can't see,
But it's very clear,
To you and me.

Lisa Michael (13)
Rainham School For Girls

CHILDREN IN NEED

Children in need,
Always need help,
For food and drink
And somewhere to stay.

Children in need,
Need to be kept warm,
They need to do some education,
In a school for something to do.

Children in need,
They struggle in pain,
Some die every day
They all hope to stay alive.

Debbie Thornton (11)
Rainham School For Girls

POOR CHILDREN

The homeless children who walk along the streets,
Who are too cold and hungry to play on their own.

They are sad and lonely,
Having nothing to do,
Think of the ones who have to work
And what they have to do.

Think of the ones who don't go to school and don't work,
Think how they feel, what can we do?

Kira Hammond (11)
Rainham School For Girls

CHILDREN IN NEED

In many countries children starve,
They are searching for food, or even beg,
Many live in boxes,
Abandoned on the streets,
Many have no parents
They only want a few sweets.

Standing there in pouring rain,
Falling over in such pain,
Having to work for some money
Children in the town are barely alive,
They have no doctor or nurse,
Many are dying, the rest are already dead.

The charities are helping so much,
Saved so many and will not give up,
Children in the boxes are only skin and bones,
They want to eat or even drink,
Some have no help, they will soon die.

Kylie Hancock (11)
Rainham School For Girls

THE AUTUMN WIND

The autumn wind is blowing fast,
Making all the leaves run past,
The gold colours glowing in the sun,
Like a fire in the sky.
Acorns bouncing on the ground,
Squirrels running round and round
Because autumn's coming
And summer's going.

Katie Dearden (11)
Rainham School For Girls

WE CAN HELP

I feel sorry you have no food to eat
No bed to lie in
No clothes to wear just old rags
All year through
We can help everyone of you!

I feel sorry for you living like you do
Begging for food, you poor things
You get thinner day by day
Let us help you, you know we can!

I feel sorry for your family
Your feet must be cold
Bruised and cut
Let us get you some shoes
For winter, you'll be cold
Please let us help!

Emma Henthorn (11)
Rainham School For Girls

ALL ABOUT AUTUMN

The leaves are red
The wind is strong
Everyone is hurrying along
It's so chilly,
It's so cold,
All the leaves are turning gold,
The grass is waving in the wind
I wish it was night
When I'm warm in my bed.

Nicola Palfreyman (11)
Rainham School For Girls

LONELY

Sitting alone day by day,
Nothing to do just sit there and pray,
Pray for some food,
Pray for a life.

Crying alone in the dark under your sheet,
Crying for light and heat,
Crying for your mum,
Crying for your dad.

Eating junk food from a rubbish pit,
Finding something to eat,
Nothing to drink,
Nothing to eat.

Maybe tomorrow I will have a life,
Maybe tomorrow I can drink,
Maybe tomorrow I can eat,
Maybe tomorrow just maybe.

Alisa Webb (12)
Rainham School For Girls

IF I WERE . . .

If I were a colour, I'd be a nice bright green
If I were a food, I would be a hot spicy curry, ready to do the salsa.
If I were a car, I'd be an MG racing through the town
If I were an animal, I'd be a horse galloping in a field
If I were a flower, I'd be a nice bold sunflower
If I were an object, I'd be a flower brightening up the day
If I were a name, I'd be a Daisy, sweet and light,
If I were . . .

Emily Edwards (13)
Rainham School For Girls

DISEASED CHILDREN

Skinny body
With bones you can see
Beady eyes
They are diseased.

In boxes they sit there
People do not dare to go near
As diseases are catching
They are diseased.

Begging is what they do
Hoping it will be a lucky day
Sometimes they get an apple or two
They throw it from a distance
They don't go near, as
They are diseased.

In the cold
Frost bitten feet
Can't move their toes
As they are frozen
That's what happens, when
They are diseased.

Michelle Ambrose (11)
Rainham School For Girls

AUTUMN

Red, yellow, gold and green means autumn has come past spring,
Leaves are falling off the trees making paths look
Gold, looking like bright golden keys.
Nuts are falling off the trees making nuts crack
When they touch the golden ground.

Stacey Moore (11)
Rainham School For Girls

HUNGRY CHILDREN

Hungry children begging on the streets
Hoping, wishing for a morsel to eat.

Hungry children begging for clothes
'Please' they say some say 'No'
Others may help and give them warm clothes
What must it feel like
No one knows.

We have lots of things, they hope for and lots
Of things that would help them,
When we waste food they would eat it gratefully.

Lots of diseases, no one to help
Most of them children how do they cope?

We could help them and give to charity shops
And give those children a future.

Lisa Ash (11)
Rainham School For Girls

HOMELESS

Why are some children homeless?
Why are we lucky and they are not?
Their homes have gone.
Our still stand
They have nowhere to go.

Cold at night and hungry in the morning
No blankets, no clean clothes,
Nothing left,
Nothing.

Emma Johnson (11)
Rainham School For Girls

SAVE THE CHILDREN!

Poor starving children,
With no home to go to.
Poor starving children,
With no school.
No food to eat,
Only dirty water to drink,
Dirty clothes, no shoes,
You are so thin.

Save the children!

Poor starving children,
Searching for food.
Drinking water that could kill.
Deadly diseases,
Slow, painful deaths.
No doctor to go to
You will soon be
Dead.

Laura Lodge (11)
Rainham School For Girls

CHILDREN IN NEED

Come care for me.
But before you judge me,
Try hard to love me,
Then you'll hug me,
Stop my heart from aching,
Stop my tears from breaking.
Look within your heart
And we'll never be apart.

Kerry King (15)
Rainham School For Girls

MY DREAM FRIEND

The trees were waving,
The sky was dull,
The sky was crying,
The clouds were low.
Down came a spaceship
From the sky,
The doors opened and
There he lies.
A big purple alien
With bulging eyes,
His feet and hands were quite a size.
I stood in front of him quite astonished,
He looked really funny to be honest.

Then he turned to me
And said with a smile,
'Have you got a drink
I've been travelling for miles.'
The way he drank it
I thought it was queer,
As I took a look
He poured it in his ear.
Then he said to me with a sigh,
'Now I've got to say goodbye.'
As the spaceship flew up to the sky,
I waved to my friend and said goodbye.
The trees were waving,
The sky was dull.
The sky was crying
The clouds were low.

Nikki Jones (13)
Rainham School For Girls

CHILDREN IN NEED

I am lucky
I've got enough food
Other people aren't so lucky
They sit and stare.

I am lucky
I've got clothes to keep me warm
Other people weren't so lucky
They don't have anything to wear.

I am lucky
I am really healthy
Other people aren't so lucky
They get diseases.

I am lucky
I'll stay alive a lot longer
Other people aren't so lucky
They are dying today.

Charlotte White (11)
Rainham School For Girls

HUNGRY CHILDREN

Hungry children,
Have no food,
They have no drink
And have nobody to help.

Hungry children
Have to work
They have to pick food from the floor,
They beg for food.

Hungry children
Are all skin and bone
They are sick
With no doctor.

Hungry children
Are weak
They have no strength,
They will soon die.

Victoria Belcher (11)
Rainham School For Girls

THINK OF THE CHILDREN

Think of the children
Nowhere to live.

Think of the children
Their lives are distress.

Think of the children
The diseases they catch
With no doctor to help them
No one at hand.

Think of the children
Their bones all weary
Think of the children
Who will soon be dead.

Think about the children
Who can't go to school.

Think about the children!

Stephanie Chaplin (11)
Rainham School For Girls

TELL SOMEONE!

Are you being bullied?
Don't want to get out of bed?
Are you being bullied?
If so you'd better
Get round the teachers
Office, better off
With the Head!

Are you being bullied?
Do you want help?
Are you being bullied?
Get your teacher to
Give 'em the
Belt?

Are you being bullied?
If so you have to tell!
Are you being bullied?
You do need help, go
Tell someone, don't
Be scared!

Tell someone!

Rachel Lamonby (11)
Rainham School For Girls

MONKEY

I hate it when people ping things at me
When I am swinging on the same old tree
They call me Milly but I'm not so silly
As all the monkeys in the zoo
I hate being stuffed in this rusty old cage
With crazy old monkeys
I share it with this other one
People call him Billy
They all go to him
And just leave me on my own
They feed him things
So I go over there
But they pick up stones
And throw them at me
I am fed up with the keepers
Making me do tricks
That I don't want to do
I just want to get fed
And move to my own cage with
Another monkey
Who is not as pretty as me
So I will get more attention
than any monkey in the zoo.

Lucy Brisley (12)
Rainham School For Girls

JUST THINK HOW LUCKY YOU ARE

These children have nothing to keep or share,
They have nothing to eat or drink
Everything is bare.

They have little water to keep them alive,
So just think how lucky you are that you
Can survive.

We have clothes, they have rags,
I expect you think this really drags.

So just think how lucky you are,
That you're warm in bed
And not nearly dead.

Jodie Stringer (11)
Rainham School For Girls

SAVE THE CHILDREN

Save the children
They rarely have a drink,
Food is what they need most,
Their bones stick out,
They have no doctors to cure them.

Save the children,
Disease is their worst enemy
People are dying nearly every day.
The parents have no money to buy food,
They don't even have clothes, they have rags.

Jennifer Burton (12)
Rainham School For Girls

WE HAVE, THEY DON'T

They have barely any food,
We have enough to survive on.

They don't have toys to play with,
We have loads of toys.

They have dirty water to survive on,
We have clean water to drink.

They have to walk miles to get water,
We just turn our tap on.

They have rags to wear,
We have decent clothes to wear.

Abigail Richardson (11)
Rainham School For Girls

HUNGRY CHILDREN

Hungry children,
Starving in the streets
Begging for food
Nothing to eat.

Nowhere to go
Living in the streets
Begging for clothes
To the people they meet.

Lots of diseases,
No doctor to call
Very thin bodies
Children are dying.

Sarah Newman (11)
Rainham School For Girls

CHILDREN IN NEED

Children in need,
Need help in all kinds of ways,
Why should they beg?
For their food and drink,
Why should they live the way they do?

Children in need
Suffering from diseases
They need doctors to help them survive,
Their skin dries up,
All you can see is their bones.

Children in need,
Don't need to starve to death,
Don't need to be cold on a winter's night,
They need to be healthy
And not as thin as a piece of paper.

Children in need,
Need love and comfort,
But if you cannot help,
Then soon they will be dead!

Claire Geary (11)
Rainham School For Girls

CHILDREN IN NEED

Children need food
Children need help
And to be safe and warm.

They need a doctor to see if they are OK,
Check their eyes
And what lies upon them.

Instead of school they work
As hard as they can
Just to help the people.

They all starve
Until they get fed,
Their skin is thin as paper
A disease will take over them
Sooner or later.

Holly Newland (11)
Rainham School For Girls

SAVE THE CHILDREN IN NEED

Children in need,
Why are you so hungry?
Why are you so thirsty?
Why are you so thin?

Children in need,
Why do you have no energy?
Why do your bones stick out?
Why is your skin so hard?

Children in need,
Why don't they have our help,
Why do they suffer?
Why are there no doctors?

Children in need,
These people need our help,
They need our support,
Before they all die.

Natalie Wyatt (11)
Rainham School For Girls

HALLOWE'EN

Scary costumes,
Sweets, chocolates and candy galore,
Money,
Decorations
Frogs, skeletons and pumpkins are all part of
Hallowe'en.
As kids all dressed up screaming
Down the street,
Witches are cackling,
Frogs are jumping,
Cauldrons bubbling,
Pumpkins burning
And ghosts saying boo!

'Trick or treat' the children scream
In the eyes and mind of the children
Hallowe'en gleams.
At the end of the night the
Full moon beams down on the
Cauldrons and pumpkins burning
Out and the ghosts still saying boo!

Dana-Jade Carter (12)
Rainham School For Girls

NO MONEY

No money for food,
No money for water,
No money for clothes,
No money for shoes,
No money to pay the doctor.

Jade Dover (11)
Rainham School For Girls

EVERYBODY'S MILLENNIUM

Listen to the countdown clock,
That eagerly ticks away the time.
Listen to their heartbeats,
That race with every war crime.

Celebrations at unusual places,
Marriages and births increase
But in the empty shell like towns,
No one pays tribute to the deceased.

In war torn countries,
Glasses are not held high
Teachers, women, crying children,
Now as amputees are left to die.

How selfish can we all be?
To not share a thought for those
Whose lives are dark and shallow,
As footage and newspapers show.

So when we celebrate the millennium
And exclaim our resolutions
Let's think of others in our mist
And work to seek solutions.

All that live, survive to tell the tale,
Of a world complex gone by
The future is ours to enjoy and enrich,
Everyone, everywhere, everything, so let's try.

Victoria Grace Smith (14)
Rainham School For Girls

SUFFERING CHILDREN

Suffering children
With no food to eat,
No money to buy
All babies cry.

Suffering children,
With skin so thin
And bone and blood full of diseases,
Getting closer to their deaths.

Suffering children,
Homeless and ill,
Their lives getting shorter and duller each day,
With no doctors to see.

Suffering children,
Getting poorer by the minute,
Cold and hungry.

Aqsa Khan (11)
Rainham School For Girls

POOR PEOPLE

Poor people get no food
Poor people get hungry,
Poor people get no drink
Poor people get thirsty.

Poor people have no doctors
Poor people get ill,
Poor people have no medicine
Poor people get worse.

Poor people don't get treatment
Poor people get weaker,
Poor people get even thinner,
Eventually poor people die.

These people are asking for help,
These people are begging for help,
These people need our help,
These people should get our help!

Ruth Gilby (11)
Rainham School For Girls

JILTED

Darkness is insufferable, I need light, take me to the light . . .
Why is the hour so cold? Where are the birds that once sang to me?
'Come back!' I feel so heavy. I must have at least put
On a stone. It feels cold and heavy.
So heavy and the pressure is all emphasised
In here, in my chest. It's a clump of darkness.
The air is so heavy I can hardly breathe.
I want to scream so he can hear me
If only he were closer, I would rip his petals off, one
By one and eat all the sweet nectar that makes him
Alluring so his colour and taste would be bleak . . .
Like mine . . .
He was incredible . . . He was incredibly stupid!
I could rip his wings off too, just to see how well
He copes. It's the air. It's too thick,
It's dry and musty . . . like him,
Bye. Maybe I'll see you sometime soon, in the boat.

Amber Khawaja (15)
Rainham School For Girls

SAVE CHILDREN

Save children all around
the world that sleep
on the streets and can't eat.

Why can't they eat?
Why do we ask these questions?
I know why because they don't
have enough money.

Why don't they have
Enough money?
Why?
Why?
Why?

Sarah-Dee King (11)
Rainham School For Girls

POOR CHILDREN

Poor children get no food,
Poor children get no food.

Poor children get very thirsty,
Poor children get very hungry.

Poor children are very thin,
Poor children have no doctors.

Poor children have no clothes,
Poor children dress in rags.

Poor children need help,
Poor children want us to help.

Kylie Austin (11)
Rainham School For Girls

SUFFERING CHILDREN

Suffering children,
Why haven't you got any food?
Why are you so poor?
How did you get poor?

Suffering children,
Why are you as thin as a stick?
Why?
You are sick and poor,
Why did it happen to you?

Suffering children,
Why are you in danger?
How did it happen to you?
Why?

Claire Green (11)
Rainham School For Girls

HUNGRY CHILDREN

They have no food to eat,
Only the things they grow.

Their skin is like paper
And their bones poke out.

Why don't they see a doctor?

They can't afford much or pay for food.

They have to work in the hot sun, all day long.

Rebecca Miles (11)
Rainham School For Girls

STARVING CHILDREN

Children thin and weak,
Begging on the street,
Eating little crumbs,
Nowhere to live.

Children thin and weak,
Look at yourself, bones is all you see,
You're so little but soon you'll die.

Children thin and weak,
Why won't anyone help me?
I would love to but now you're dead.

Children thin, weak and dead,
Why did you have to die like that?
Is it because no one cared about you,
Or didn't have any food spare?
Goodbye little children.

Hannah Grant (11)
Rainham School For Girls

STOP THE CHILDREN GOING HUNGRY

Stop the children going hungry
They deserve more than this
Why are they so hungry?
Buy them something to eat!

Stop the children going hungry!
Give them something to eat and drink!
We can't leave them like this?
So why don't we go and help?

Zia Whitehead (11)
Rainham School For Girls

OLD BASIL

A chestnut friend called Basil
His happy eyes twinkle when they see me
He continues to munch on his hay
I stroke his silky mane
He then replies with a gentle neigh.

I lead him to his water trough
I tell him it's time for a ride
I tighten up his girth
But he gives me a swift little bite.

Old Basil is slow
He only likes to walk
I take him to trot, with a flick of the crop
He's soon into canter, with a smooth comfy ride.

At night he goes home
To his stable in Oak Lane
He is handsome, sleek and fine
I wish he was mine.

Tanya Horne (13)
Rainham School For Girls

AUTUMN LEAVES

All the nuts lie on the ground
All the squirrels gather round
All the squirrels take them home
But then there came a horrid storm
And then the squirrels gave a warn
When you walk, you walk on leaves
And then you carry on, more begin to fall.

Shelley Collings (11)
Rainham School For Girls

My Rabbit

My rabbit hops around the garden all day long.
When he sees a cat over the fence, he sits
Up high and looks up at the sky with both of his
ears up, then when he hears and sees it, he
runs around the garden like a lunatic and runs to the door
with his ears up high.

He runs into the house and then into the kitchen where we
all stand and give him hugs and kisses. He stays in the house
If the rabbit next door is not out and then we put him away
and he sits there until he is full up with a big carrot.

Then we say goodnight and then he goes to sleep.

Sarah Sloan (12)
Rainham School For Girls

Sick Children

Sick children,
Why are you so sick?
Why is your skin so thin?

Sick children,
Why are you suffering from starvation?
Why can we see your bones?

Sick children,
Why are you so poor?
Why do you not have a home?

Sick children,
Why are you eaten up by diseases?
Why not see a doctor?

Rachel Finniss (11)
Rainham School For Girls

CAPTURED KOALA

They were coming towards me,
As I was wandering one day.
They captured me and
Took me away.
I thought I'd never see
The light of day.
They bundled me in a barred
Cage, as I tried to kick them away.
But that was then and
This is now. Oh I wish
They would have gone away.
They say they rescued me.
Rescue me?
What a joke!
People laughing,
Bundling past, I'm not laughing,
I can't bundle past.
I know I'll never forget the past.

Katy McCutcheon (12)
Rainham School For Girls

MY HAMSTER AT NIGHT

Hamster,
Hamster,
On his wheel, never still
Until morning when daylight appears.
My hamster will not stir until night reappears.

Zoey Orford (12)
Rainham School For Girls

MY DOG

I felt cold all over
My dog was run over
I thought my life was over
He was such fun to play with
I told him all my secrets
He never told anyone
When I was five, he was alive
When I saw six
He died.
He was my best friend
No other dog could replace him
He was everything I wanted
We buried him in the garden
And our love has never died.

Michaela Whittaker (12)
Rainham School For Girls

A SUMMER MORNING

The sunshine's golden
The sunshine's bright
The sky is blue and also white.
The birds fly high in the sky.
I watch them carefully
As they fly by.
The dew on leaves
Glistens in the sun.
The dew on the grass
When all is done.

Samantha Kittredge (12)
Rainham School For Girls

ALL THE FUN OF THE FAIR

Remember the fun and excitement
Remember the scare of the rides
To see the people's faces as they scream with sheer delight.
The taste of the candyfloss
The smell of the hot dog stall
The whiz of the rides going round and round
A good time had by all.

As the sun goes down
The lights beam brighter
As you step onto the waltzers
The fear of the ride makes your stomach knot tighter.

The dogdem cars bump
The octopus twirls
The big wheel spins
Boys kiss girls
Laughter rings out at the fun of the fair
People go home without even a care.

Hayley Bodkin (12)
Rainham School For Girls

THE TRAPPED TIGER

I tried to hide in the wild,
But then I saw those rotten people with a smile.
My beautiful coat caught their eyes behind
The tree, the orange shone, they scared
The living daylights out of me.
I ran for a while and there he was,
Caught me in a cage for a while.
They took me to the zoo where they left me to please.

Lauren Ramson (13)
Rainham School For Girls

THE TRAPPED GIRAFFES

The feeling of getting out of here
Is starting to fade away
Will I ever be free?
I ask myself each day.

I'm lonely, confused and frightened
What will happen to me next?
I wish I had my freedom back
I liked it that way best.

When I awake each morning
I forget just where I am
Then I stand up and see the bars
Oh no! I am still trapped
In this horrible grey tin can!

Katie Hobbs (12)
Rainham School For Girls

MY GRANDAD IS GONE, GONE AND NEVER TO COME BACK

You were the sunshine of my heart
The brightest star above
And when I thought about you
It brought a happiness to my heart.
But now that you have gone
I have to try and remember all the
Good times that we had together
And try not to remember that
You are now gone and never
To come back.

Lauren Hendry (12)
Rainham School For Girls

PETS

I have a pet dog
She's white with
Black spots,
She's a Staffordshire
Bull Terrier
But they're all
The merrier to
Watch and have
Around.

She's playful and
Bouncy just
Like a bounty
That tastes so
Good in your mouth
But when she sees
A cat she'll yell
Like a rat
'Cause she can't get
Off the lead.

She'll protect you
And cuddle you
But she'll also
Muddle you
When you're
Trying to sort
Things out.

Carla White (12)
Rainham School For Girls

SUMMER TO AUTUMN

It's mid summer's day in the middle of June,
Everyone's happy from morning till noon.
They lie in the sun for hours and hours,
While honey bees buzz around all the flowers.
Children play happily with family and friends,
They hope that the warm weather will never end.
Farmers plough fields and cut the corn,
They work so many hours from dusk till dawn.

Summer is such a lovely time,
All the plants have finished their climb.
They have bloomed so big and bold,
The sun looks like a big ball of gold.
Then all the leaves begin to fall,
From all the trees so big and tall.
All the animals scatter and hide,
To every place far and wide.

Now it's autumn, the leaves all turn brown,
Whether they're in the country or whether in town.
People wrap up in all their thick clothes,
They cook big hot dinners on their gas stoves.
The rain begins to fall again more and more each day,
The flowers die and the skies become dull, bleak and grey.

Nicola Carver (12)
Rainham School For Girls

MY DOG BARKS

If a dog barks loud
And clear, you might
Hear it here, and there
Or anywhere, if you
Do be sure to know.

My dog knows something
You don't know, you might
Want to go out and check,
You never know, he might
Have a cat by the neck.

Montana Burch (13)
Rainham School For Girls

FREEDOM

Splashing around under the sea,
So happily,
> Set me free.
> Set me free.

Then came a ship, I tried to escape,
But they got me,
> Set me free.
> Set me free.

I am a prisoner, the endless routine,
Of splashing in and out of rings,
> Set me free.
> Set me free.

People staring at me,
Look at that dolphin,
> Set me free.
> Set me free.

I know I shall never be free,
With no way in and no way out,
> Set me free.
> Set me free.

Natasha Ford (12)
Rainham School For Girls

LADS PLAY FOOTIE

On Sunday the lads play football at Strood,
Though lots of them go home in a mood,
With their fab attempts to win,
All their great talent is thrown in the bin,
I would like to participate in this wonderful game,
Though some lads kick you to death not mentioning a name,
Their strip can be either colour or white,
But they play through hailstones and on a very dark night,
The best players are Nathan, Matt, Dion, Saul and Dad,
But sometimes they get into a stupid angry pad,
Nathan's meant to be teaching me footie one day,
I suppose as I'm rubbish he'd expect me to pay,
All you can hear is them saying 'over here'
While I'm being deafened as I'm sitting very near,
If you are watching be prepared to be hit,
But you can go in the pub to have a drink and a nice long sit,
One day I'll be on the pitch scoring many goals,
I'll be a professional just like Paul Scholes.

__Leanne Lawson (12)__
__Rainham School For Girls__

PRISON

Here I am,
All alone,
Only iron bars,
As company.

I look through a gap,
To find my friends
But all I can see are people staring at me!

I don't understand
What have I done to deserve this?
Where is my son?
I can hear him cry!

Will someone save me
From my prison?

Nicola Wall (12)
Rainham School For Girls

POPULAR POLAR BEAR

Swimming in the cold salt water,
Passed the shimmering glass
Looking at all the faces
Again and again and again.

Up I jump onto the
Soft, warm snow
Trying to hide behind the trees,
Looking at all the faces
Again and again and again.

Sleeping on my
Thin straw bed
Open to all the world.
Looking at all the faces
Again and again and again.

Sitting on a cold, wet floor
Shivering under my fur
My eyes close
I don't wake up
No more of those faces
Again and again and again.

Natalie Thomson (12)
Rainham School For Girls

I Want To Be Free

I was a tiger in the open,
Roaming freely, every day
Catching my own fresh food
When all of a sudden a net.

Now I'm such a lonely tiger
No friends to play with
Eating meat, days old
And bars all around me!

Am I ever going to get out?
Please let me go!
I haven't done anything to you!
Let me go! I want to be free!

Charlotte Pullen (12)
Rainham School For Girls

Autumn Is Here

Autumn's here, leaves are falling,
Falling in colours red, gold and green.
It is so cold now for summer has gone
And the weather is being mean.
But there is lots to look forward to
The red squirrel running with chestnuts
In its mouth, the Guy Fawkes Night with
Fireworks spraying wonderful colours, the long
Winter nights snuggled up in your bed,
Autumn is here, autumn is here!

Ashleigh Crozier (12)
Rainham School For Girls

I REMEMBER . . .

I remember when I was born
It was just before dawn
I remember my first dog
It always chewed logs.

I remember my first bike
It got punched by a spike
I remember my first house
It didn't have any mouse.

I remember my second dog
That was the day that it was thick with fog
I remember my first day at school
The teachers didn't think I was a fool.

I remember my SATs
Where we weren't allowed to wear hats
I remember my first day at secondary school
We weren't allowed to play football.

Becky Creavin (14)
Rainham School For Girls

I USED TO . . .

I used to be a tiger running the open plains,
Now I'm just an object being looked at every day.

I used to catch my own food in the water or long grass,
Now they feed me rotten meat I haven't got a chance!

When I go to sleep at night I dream of pastures new,
I really wish I could be free of this cage and awful zoo!

Katie Christy (13)
Rainham School For Girls

TRAPPED BEHIND BARS

In the jungle I would roam,
Now I have been taken from my home,
To be stared at and talked about,
By the people who don't care.

Don't they understand, I have a family,
Who needs looking after,
I get fed rotten meat
And they get ice-cream and treats.

My little babe I hear his cry
The cry of a starving cub,
Let me out! Let me save him!
Oh please, I want my cub.

All those children say
I want her to roam,
But I just ignore those words
And wish that I'll be freed,
One day I will! I promise!

Hannah Jordan (12)
Rainham School For Girls

THE PANDA

Sitting behind the tall black bars,
Gazing into the sky.
All day long I say to myself,
Try not to cry!
They might have put you here
For a reason, you know,
Maybe I could be safe,
No, I just want to go home!

Chains and bars all around me
People stand and stare,
Walking by and pointing
At this sad and lonely panda bear.
I want to be with my family,
I want to be with my friends,
Not locked up on my own,
Yes, all alone!

Laura Mittoo (12)
Rainham School For Girls

THE ORANG-UTAN

I'm here in this rotten old cage,
Just sitting in the corner.
Wishing that I'd just be let out for one hour.
Let me out, let me out, let me out!

I want to be free, I want to swing
From tree to tree,
I won't do any harm
Let me out, let me out, please let me out!

Right, I know what I am going to do,
When he opens up the door to give me my food,
I'm going to run out, run out, then I'd be free,
I'm going to get out. get out, get out!

Now I'm gonna get out,
Even if I have to scream and shout,
But oh no, he's just thrown the food in,
I've just got no chance, no chance,
No chance!

Natalie Coker (12)
Rainham School For Girls

I Miss My Dad

For those of you who have a dad,
Love him while you may,
Because I know with all my heart
I wish I had mine today.
So don't ever let go because
The pain doesn't fade away.
It's kinda hard when he's not around
Knowing he's in heaven smiling down.
That cold feeling inside me,
That won't break through.
It has really touched me,
As much it will touch you.
My dad was always there,
He would take me everywhere,
I'll never see him again,
I really miss him you know.
But very deep inside me,
He will come back to contact me,
He will always remember me
And have a soft spot for me,
Forget those silly arguments,
Forget the days he grounded you,
Because all these things only
Happen because he loves you!

Elisabeth Martin (12)
Rainham School For Girls

The Miserable Dolphin

I gazed at all those delighted people
I wish I felt like that!
They stared at me and I stared at them
I circled around and around in my empty aquarium,
Everything and all the people were blurred.

I felt my tiny pupils dilating,
Looking at the circular hoop with the blazing fire,
How can they make me leap through that?
I felt a cold shiver down my spine
My life began to sink within my sad and lonely heart.

Leanne Friday (12)
Rainham School For Girls

THE STREETS

Beady eyes looking up at you
Please help us!
Please help us!

They sit there begging, begging.
Nobody seems to notice them,
Some just cross the road,
Others will throw them a penny or two,
And that penny is like gold
To the poor children on the streets.

Children scuttle into their tiny little boxes
As the rain starts to fall
They squeeze up tight
For the cold air can give a nasty chill.

But some just sit there
Because some have already got
Killing diseases and are going to die anyway,
So what is a little chill going to do?

Beady eyes looking up at you
Please help us!
Please help us!

Stacey Purcell (11)
Rainham School For Girls

MY HEART WILL GO ON

I didn't really understand
About death and the panic,
Until I went to see the film
All about Titanic.

They called it the ship of dreams
Until they had that awful crash,
The boat starting to tilt
Making people dash.

Women and children go first
As they lower the boats,
It's dark and really cold
Is there any sign of hope?

Hundreds of people died that night
No one will ever know,
For the ones who survived
The pain will never go.

Kelly Reavill (13)
Rainham School For Girls

HOUSES

Houses big!
Houses small!
Houses wide!
Houses tall!

John's house is big
And Clare's is small!
Vicky's is wide,
And Leanne's is tall!

But I don't have a house
I live on a street
All alone,
With nothing to eat!

But this doesn't matter,
'Cause today I'll survive
I'm just happy
To be alive!

Francesca Miseldine (12)
Rainham School For Girls

SUFFERING CHILDREN

Children are suffering
With no food or homes
Why do they suffer?
Why do they cry?

Children suffer because
They have no clothes
They're scared to drink
Water from wells because
They cause disease.

Children suffer because
Their mothers
Are scared to feed
They think the dirty water will kill them.

Why?

Kirandeep Basi (11)
Rainham School For Girls

BLACK HALLOWE'EN

Black is the night
Black is the cat
That sat on the witches mat
With the wind blowing
And the fire glowing
So cosy on the mat.

Black is the night
Black is the pot
With bubbles boiling and witches drooling
And overcastting spells.

Black is the night
Black is the night
And full moon shines down
With a rap at the door and children galore
With trick or treat in mind.

Black is the night
That gave them a fright
When the witch was unkind
With an almighty yell
She cackled a spell that made them unwell
That they were unable to spell or to tell
What a haunting Hallowe'en they had!

Sarah Grimes (12)
Rainham School For Girls

A TIGER POEM

I hate this place
I want to be free
To roam across the grassy ground
To play and to chase
I just need to be free.

Every day I see the bars that keep me locked up
And people looking up at me
They always come and go
Why can't I wander around
But instead I am in this cage!

Sian Olsen (12)
Rainham School For Girls

A SADDENED OLD SEAL

I was roaming freely
And all of a sudden I was caught
And taken to captivity
I was shut in a cage
With no one to see
Except a smelly ball they left me.

My nose is sore
From the rubber ball
Which was balanced on my nose
So I could be put on display
To the public which come today.

They hit me with sticks
Why are they so cruel?
I never hurt them at all.

I have a pain in my heart
And a sadness in my eye
I cry and cry
For my mum and dad
Who were taken away
And treated badly.

Lauren A'Court (13)
Rainham School For Girls

RSPCA - ANIMALS IN NEED

Walk in my first impression
Fear and illness
Walk out
Ill treatment, death and neglect
It's not fair, no, no, no!

Walk in
Smell and starvation
Walk out
I can't bear to look
It's not fair, no, no, no!

Walk in
Love and joy
Walk out
Freedom and food
That's better, yes, yes, yes!

Royal Society for the Prevention of Cruelty to Animals.

Chloe Dungey (11)
Rainham School For Girls

THE ELEPHANT

I am so tall
I do not belong in the zoo
My trunk is long
I do not belong in the zoo
My hopes sometimes live
But they sink as another child
Looks into my cage.
I dream of being free
I do not belong in the zoo.

Claire Casterton (12)
Rainham School For Girls

FREEDOM!

Why did it happen to me?
Born in captivity.
I long to play out in the wild,
But that won't happen to me, not for a while.

I spray the water from the lake,
It helps me to wake.
Beyond the bars you just laugh,
You think I like it but not me
I'm just here to bathe.

Elephants here long to be free,
Like us, my family and me.
My hopes are high that I'll be free,
But not me I'll never be free.

Corinne Walden (12)
Rainham School For Girls

THE I WISH POEM

I wish I had a shelter,
I wish I had food,
I wish I had clothes,
I wish I had a mum and dad,
Someone who loves me,
I wish I had a brother or sister,
To love and keep me happy,
I wish I had some shoes,
And some nice soft feet,
I wish for one thing to go to school
Get an education and to make some new
And nice caring friends.

Kirsty McDougall (11)
Rainham School For Girls

CAGED IN

I used to be a monkey
Climbing in the trees
Now I'm in a zoo
With people watching me.

Swinging on ropes
In a little cage
That seems to get smaller
Day by day.

Seeing people come and go
I wish that it was me
To just see all my friends again
Would make me laugh and scream.

Amy Sterba (13)
Rainham School For Girls

THE LEOPARD

Unhappy, downhearted and sad,
Bored, miserable and lonely,
Confined and missing my home
Oh! I wish they had left me alone!

Free, happy and excited,
Loved, joyful and merry,
Falling asleep under the stars
But here all I see is metal bars!

I know I'll never escape here,
Until I come to my end
Just wishing and wanting home
Oh! I wish they had left me alone!

Amy Kisby (12)
Rainham School For Girls

CHILDREN IN NEED!

Children should be happy
They should not get slappy's.

Children are special things they
Are fragile like China.

They don't like being hit or lit and
Don't blame them if they have a fit.

Children should be loved by their
Parents and just remember to
Look
After
Your
Children!

Gemma Cole (11)
Rainham School For Girls

LIFELESS CHILDREN

Lifeless children,
Why did you drink that water
When you knew it was dirty?

Lifeless children,
Why did you eat that food
When you knew it was old and dirty?

Lifeless children,
I like you and I'll try to help.

Lifeless children,
Next thing they know, you're dead.

Erica Wilson (11)
Rainham School For Girls

MONKEY ENTRAPMENT

I'm not very happy
Just walking around all day
Please, please, please,
I want to get away!

Running, jumping, swinging, climbing
That's all I want to do
In the forest where I belong
Not in this horrible zoo!

People watching all the time
Always shouting things at me
Wanting me to do some tricks
Can't they see I want to be
Free!

Emma Pollett (12)
Rainham School For Girls

NSPCC

Where's my mum and dad?
Where are my brothers and sisters?
Why are these tubes in me?

Why can't I play with my toys?
Why can't I drink warm milk?
Why can't I be hugged?

Why am I wearing these funny clothes?
Why am I stuck in this wired place?
Why am I in here? Why? Why? Why?

Rachel Toombs (11)
Rainham School For Girls

CHILDREN IN NEED

Charities
People need money,
Have no food,
Have no house
To live in.

Charities
They cannot walk,
Can't see the doctor
To see what is wrong
With them,
They don't have many family.

Charities
They have disease
They will soon be dead.

Kelly Bessell (11)
Rainham School For Girls

ANIMALS IN NEED!

Animals need their mum,
Naughty children hurt others
I have pets of my own and I look after them,
Mammals are very nice,
All animals should be treated the same,
I would look after all animals,
So should every one else.

Samantha Louise Binfield (11)
Rainham School For Girls

WATERLESS CHILDREN

Waterless children,
With stomachs puffed out
Why have you no water to drink?

Why have you no water from taps?
Waterless children,
Suffering from disease.

Why are you so thin?

Waterless children
Driven up by disease
Why not see a doctor?
Why not?

Waterless children
You are so thin,
Your body is fading
And you will soon be dead!

Colette Pascal (11)
Rainham School For Girls

DEMELZA HOUSE

I am in a place,
Where I am not going home.
I am staying here,
Till I die.
It's not a nice thought but I will
That's why I am here.
They have lots of fun
Here, they also have lots
Of cuddly toys.

Laura Harley (11)
Rainham School For Girls

HOMESICK DOLPHIN

I remember what life was like,
In the deep blue sea
I hate people looking and staring at me
I wish I was set free,
Back to the deep blue sea.

I wish I could see my family again,
They always loved me
I wish I could be set free
Back into the deep blue sea.

The people don't know how I feel,
I wish this wasn't real,
I wish I could be set free,
Back to the deep blue sea.

Suzanne Mills (12)
Rainham School For Girls

CLAIRE'S SOS

They scream like mad
Everyone moping and are very sad,
People shouting like mad,
Some are good, some are bad.
Some are very happy to be loved and are very glad,
Having things they have never had
Holding tight to their dad.

When they think there is no end,
They find themselves going around the bend
And things they ask to lend
And things they want to send.

Claire Louise Webb (11)
Rainham School For Girls

THE OTTER

As I look around my home
All it is, is a bit of ground with
Glass around it.
When I look at the glass all
I can see is myself.

People look at me
As if it is funny.
But 'tis just me
A friendly little otter.

I have my friend with me.
But he is quite old
And can't do much
So he is not much fun.

I wish I was free.

Laura Hanniford (12)
Rainham School For Girls

FOR THE PEOPLE IN NEED

I ask of you to send things to the
Hungry and poor,
Just a little money to help them
Get through the day.

I ask of you to send things to the
Hungry and poor,
Who walk miles and miles just to get drink
Drink that can kill them and their children.

I ask of you to send things to the
Hungry and poor,
Who have no food to eat or anything to survive on,
Who can't grow anything because it is too hot.

I ask of you to send things to the
Hungry and poor,
Give them a chance and contribute some money,
Please help the NSPCC.

Gemma Turner (11)
Rainham School For Girls

TIRED TIGER

I have walked these bars
A million times
Looking, staring, thinking.
My ears go up
Every time someone goes past
Wishing they'd set me free.

My feet are all black and grubby
They only wash me once a week.
People look at me
As though I am
Some kind of freak.

There are times that
I am glad to be here
When it is raining and snowing
Or cold and windy
But I mostly wish I was
With my friends and family.

Louise Grant (12)
Rainham School For Girls

FOODLESS CHILDREN

Foodless children
cannot eat
Foodless children
cannot drink
Foodless children
cannot sleep
Foodless children
have bare feet
Foodless children
are asleep
Foodless children
are so thin
Foodless children.

Foodless children
are so cold.
Foodless children
are crying
Foodless children
are dying.

Amanda Conquest (11)
Rainham School For Girls

ANIMALS IN NEED

A   nimals are suffering
N   o one is hardly doing anything about it
I   t is important that we care for animals
M   any animals need our help
A   s animals are being born all over the world animals are being born
L   iving animals have the right to live
S   o let animals get rid of their illness by a special cure.

Katrina Gordon (11)
Rainham School For Girls

MY LIFE

My amber eyes shut tight,
Imagining the jungle's beams of concealed light,
The grasses rustle and the
air is filled with unusual scents.

My camouflaged body lies hidden, waiting, for that
moment when I need to pounce on some
unexpected pray.

But it's not to be
The beams of light are just shadows.
Sunlight filtering through the rusty bars of hell.
There is no leafy canopy overhead.

A small cramped cage imprisons me.
My beautiful pelt is my only crime
People's greed is responsible for my plight.

Alyshia Abramian (13)
Rainham School For Girls

DOLPHIN POEM

I have a huge tank
But I want to be free
I want to live out in the ocean with my family.
I cry to them every lonely night
This place is horrible,
I have to play silly tricks for all those people,
When all I get is a piece of fish,
I want to be free to catch it myself,
I want to be free.

Zoe Newman (12)
Rainham School For Girls

THE NEVER FREE EAGLE

Sit, never fly, never hunt
Never will I feel the wind on my feathers
Never will I see the evergreen
Never will I see the sapphire sky
Never will I feel the heat of the sun
Never will I feel the fresh kill in my claws
Never will I see my reflection in clear waters
Never will I feel the cold of the rocky cliffs
Never will I feel the twigs in my nest.

>Never never
>Never will I be

>*Free!*

Sheona Walsh (12)
Rainham School For Girls

IN MY WORLD

In my world there would be peace
In my world there would be no more crying,
In my world people would always be smiling,
In my world there would be no famine or droughts
In my world there would be no dead bodies about,
In my world nobody would care about anybody's skin colour.
In my world what would count comes from within.
In my world there would always be pure flowing water,
In my world every adult would have sons and daughters,
In my world there would be fun in the sun for everyone,
Old or young I knew they would have fun.

Tosin Temitope Odubanjo (13)
Rainham School For Girls

THE MONKEY

I am tired of swinging
On the same old bits
Of rope and branches.

I am sick of fighting
With the same old monkeys.
I am bored with being
Stuck in this old cage
Not being able to go
Where I want in the jungle.

I am brain-dead
From having to do
All these stupid tricks.

I am asking you now
Before it's too late
Let me out
Oh please let me out!

Lea Harrington (12)
Rainham School For Girls

AUTUMN'S COME

Autumn leaves flying by, the autumn sun it burns my eye.
The leaves have fallen on the ground,
They all shine brightly, they make me frown
The rain is falling on the ground, the coloured leaves fly all about.
I walk down the swirling street and see the squirrels eat.
The night has come and the wind is howling,
It's very strong, and now there is no burning sun.

Melissa Cass (11)
Rainham School For Girls

RSPCA

Homeless animals
make me sad
been left alone
by themselves.

Homeless animals
with no one to look after them
and nowhere to go
why, why are you like this?

Then RSPCA
came, then they
have someone to look after them
and somewhere to go.
Then they have a new life.

Sophie Jimenez (11)
Rainham School For Girls

TIGERS

I am a tiger
I look very frightening
Inside I wouldn't hurt a fly.

But then I get taken from my home
and put in these small little places
With barely any food to eat.

People sometimes look and laugh
and say 'Tigers are so mean.'
But inside I wouldn't hurt a fly.

Leanne Britton (12)
Rainham School For Girls

DOLPHIN'S DREAM

I see all the eyes gazing at me,
like I am a non-living creature.
I get to have a little joy,
not a lot,
jumping through hoops,
playing with me like I am a doll.

I remember to have fun, swimming
around an ocean, not a cage!
They have destroyed my way of living.
All I have is a dream that won't ever come true.

I could see myself in the ocean, living where I desire.
The world is my home, not a little tank.
I can only dream about being free.
The only truth is that
I am going to die
in my own little dream.

Rachel Hicks (12)
Rainham School For Girls

AUTUMN LEAVES

Autumn comes and autumn goes,
History is going really slow.

All the colours are really neat,
Especially when they go under my feet.

The fun is finished and now it's all gone,
So really it's like a really big song.

Naomi Morrow (12)
Rainham School For Girls

ANIMALS' RESPECT

Animals are treated cruelly nearly every day.
You should treat your pets as you treat yourselves.
We should respect animals,
Look after and feed them well.
You shouldn't let them starve, roaming streets
Help and look after and respect animals.

Hayley Castle (11)
Rainham School For Girls

AUTUMN

In the autumn when it's dark
You won't see a swallow or a lark
The only thing that you will see
Are leaves that are falling, coming towards me
But the wind is howling all around
As leaves begin to cover the ground.

Emily Martin (11)
Rainham School For Girls

AUTUMN IS NEAR

Autumn's near as you can hear
The wind is howling
The leaves are falling.
The birds are flying.
I start to cry, I can't see the blue sky.

Jennie Dodds (11)
Rainham School For Girls

HELP

I hear
I hear the poor calling
'Help, help' and a long sobbing 'Please'
'I hear you calling
I will try
I will try'
I say back
'But I cannot do it alone.'
There are children dying, diseases spreading.
You can help. *Please help.*
'How?'
By buying clothes and things for charities.
You don't even have to go into the shop, put it in a charity box.

Oh help. It will make a difference!

Martyne Wheeler (11)
Rainham School For Girls

AUTUMN'S COMING

Autumn's coming, leaves are falling,
Leaves are changing red and brown,
The wind blows the branches about,
The sun has gone high in the sky,
People moan about all of this,
But some people think it's magic,
Branches are waving at you,
So autumn's coming, autumn's coming,
Don't stay indoors, come outside,
Have some fun and do not hide.

Gemma Dicker (11)
Rainham School For Girls

AUTUMN

Autumn is so great,
While the dead beautiful coloured leaves fall,
It's so magical and real,
I just can't wait.

Yellow, red, gold and brown leaves,
Fall and cover the ground,
As you walk over the coloured leaves,
Some more fall off trees.

A sprinkle of wind fills the air,
And a squirrel jumps from branch to branch,
Look around at the leaves and imagine new colours beginning,
Just look at the leaves there.

The sun makes the leaves sparkle and shine,
And the rain from last night drips,
The leaves on the ground are wet then dried by the sun,
So just remember the magical and beautiful autumn is here.

Grace Gallacher (11)
Rainham School For Girls

AUTUMN IS HERE

Wind whistling through my hair,
Leaves twirling, turning, swirling,
Trees swaying in the breeze,
Squirrels running collecting nuts,
Children playing, having fun,
Autumn is here, spring has gone.

Joanne Sargent (11)
Rainham School For Girls

GIVE THE HUNGRY CHILDREN

Give the hungry children
a place where they can sleep.
Give the hungry children
a different way to live.

Help our hungry children
to live their little lives.
Help our hungry children
to go to school and revise.

Give the hungry children
a better way to learn.
Give the hungry children
some money so they can live.

Save the hungry children,
Save the hungry children.

Sophia Tuck-Brown (11)
Rainham School For Girls

AUTUMN

Autumn leaves rushing past, red, yellow and brown.
Autumn's here, summer's gone. Leaves are falling, the sun has died.
Children have gone back inside,
Won't come to play outside,
Autumn's here, summer's gone,
Bye faye pinkney sun, summer's gone.

Trudi Wallis (11)
Rainham School For Girls

THE LONELY DOLPHIN

I am alone in a place.
That I do not know,
On my own with no one to care
They just stare
I am tired and lonely,
No one is my type,
Lions growl and scare me
Why? I ask why?
I am in a pond by myself,
I can't be warm, I'm just shivering,
There is nothing to live for anymore,
I just wish that I would die!
Or I already have in my heart.
I can no longer be happy!

Gillian Pain (13)
Rainham School For Girls

CHILDREN IN NEED

Quickly help these
children, they need
your help.
They have nothing
to eat and drink,
so send them
what you can.
Charities, you must
help them before
it's too late.

Carla Smith (11)
Rainham School For Girls

POP STAR POEM

I would like to be a pop star
And get up on stage
And sing really nicely at such a young age
All of my life I've wanted it to come true
And it might.
If I keep singing day and night.
Being a pop star is a big thing.
Getting up on stage and having to sing.
Loads of fans will come and go.
And loads of managers swinging to and fro.
You will need to look your best
When you have a photo
You don't want to look horrible for your first solo.
Kids would want your autograph so what do you do?
Sign their books and say that's for you.
Concerts oh concerts there will be loads
People are asking for addresses and codes
If only I could sing I could be a pop star
So I should hurry up and do what I've got to do.
And I could be travelling.
Very very far.

Amy Wilmot (15)
Rowhill School

MUSIC

Music is cool
Music is mean
Music is loud
And mystic is groovy
And head banging
Music has loud drums

Dean Wright (15)
Rowhill School

LONDON LIFE

Busy London life hits you like a knife,
Busy London life is full of strife.
Busy London life is hustling and bustling
with commuters and computers.
Busy London life is full of shops to make a quick stop
to buy flashy and classy clothes.
Busy London life is dusty, with workmen planning
and building new buildings like offices.
Busy London life has policemen,
waiting to give you some advice.
Busy London life has spacious parks -
No! Or shouldn't it be like this?
No London life hitting you like a knife,
No London life filled with strife.
No London life hustling and bustling
with commuters with computers.
No London life dusty with workmen
No London life with policemen to ask advice
No, I just want London to be filled with parks,
and after it gets dark, people can come and walk their dogs.
Also, I prefer on New Year's Day at twelve o'clock (midnight)
a quiet London with Big Ben chiming over a new millennium.
To welcome in the new millennium.
It will be just me riding around on an open-topped bus.
With Big Ben chiming in the distance to welcome
in the millennium to the whole wide world.

Emma Davies (13)
Rowhill School

LOVE POEM

I look out of my window and what do I see?
I see a lovely girl staring at me.
She had a lovely golden smile
She gave me a kiss and waved goodbye.
Not for now and not for ever.

I woke up in the morning and what did I see?
I saw that lovely girl standing next to me.
I asked for her name
Her name was Caroline (who was sitting next to me).
She asked me my name
My name is David.
Did they make a go of it . . . !

David Peach (15) & Simon Knapp (15)
Rowhill School

ONE DAY IN THE HOUSE

One day in a house lived a fat cat ,
And called it a little fat rat.
It was always on the run for a little bun.
Then the little fat rat,
Went flat flat flat
I am a rat.
They called me fat because I am a little rat
But then I went skinny like a little mouse
Then they called me skinny.
Skinny go back to your binny.

Jamie Taylor (14)
Rowhill School

BONFIRE

Hear the bang that crackles in the night
And whistles in the day
And everyone is cheering for the fireworks
And hears a loud bang
The rocket went up in the sky
And it's so steamy and cloudy and raining
And the bonfire is going out
So that is the end of the bonfire
And everyone is whistling.

Sharon Oakley (14)
Rowhill School

2100

I believe there is going to be more technology
Like more computers to sort out the knowledge
Of the young and old people
When young and old get stuck just use a computer
For information to help your career
People will make robots and get the information for a computer.
I think that computers will take over the world.
The people will get their information from a computer.
Don't you agree?

Michael Carey (14)
St Anthony's Special School, Margate

THE EARTH PEOPLE

There will be lots of pirates
On an island
On an island
They will dig, dig, for gold

Robots will go to the island
They will say we are robots
They will attack the pirates
And take over

Aliens come from outer space
They will live under water
They will be small
They will be tall

Computers will take over
Things will begin to change
Schools need no teachers
Children teach themselves.

Georgina Parker (14)
St Anthony's Special School, Margate

BITS AND BOBS

The aliens are going to be small and tall
They will have one eye
They will bring new technology
And new ships
But they will die off
Because the air is not right.

One day aliens bring back
A pile of metal
The man has to make a robot
The technology could make it digital
He needs extra parts.

There is now no teachers
The students watch the screen
It's all become digital
No one around to see
All we do is watch the box
And information fill our ears.

Chevy Crompton (14)
St Anthony's Special School, Margate

ALIENS!

Some people think I'm crazy
That there isn't anything out there!
But as I look at the star-studded sky
I think to myself 'What if?'

What if there were aliens in flying saucers?
What if they were looking down on us?
What if they were planning to attack?
What could we do to get them back?

Some people think I'm stupid
That there isn't anything out there
But as I look at the star-studded sky
I think to myself 'Why! Oh why?'

Why would they be in a flying saucers?
Why would they be looking down?
Why would they be planning an attack?
And why would we want to get them back?

Corinne Hastings (13)
St Mary & St Joseph's School, Sidcup

I SEEM TO BE BUT . . .

I seem to be small but others are just too tall
I seem to be shy but I am very loud
I seem to be bossy but I just want things to be perfect
I seem to be lazy but I just take time in things
I seem to be nosy but I just care about other people
I seem to be different but really I am special.

Katie Edwardes (12)
St Mary & St Joseph's School, Sidcup

THE PAPER CLIP (CONVENIENCE)

Slender, silver paper clip
clinging to each little slip
what immortal hand or eye
devised your round edged symmetry?

In what distant office room
did a man await his doom
to die under a paper pile
because he simply could not file?

But what shoulder and what form
can't twist you like a silver worm?
What a delicate thing thou art
but how useful and how smart.

What the memo? What the note?
What thing is there that man has wrote
that could escape your slender clasp
which brings about a vice-like grasp?

When secretaries start careers
who stopped them breaking into tears?
Did he smile his work to see?
Did he who made the Bic make thee?

Slender, silver paper clip
clinging to each little slip
what immortal hand or eye
devised your round edged symmetry?

Nick Smith (15)
St Mary & St Joseph's School, Sidcup

Isn't It A Wonder?

Isn't it a wonder how the sky
goes from blue to black.

Isn't it a wonder how the sunsets
and the moon rises.

Isn't it a wonder how the stars
twinkle so bright.

Isn't it a wonder that the Earth
moves round and round.

Isn't it a wonder that the sun
is a star in the daytime.

Isn't it a wonder that the planets
may have life on them.

I guess I'll never really know
because everything's a wonder?

Joanna Gallardo (12)
St Mary & St Joseph's School, Sidcup

I Seem To Be But . . .

I seem to be different but I'm really the same
I seem to be mad but really I'm sane
I seem to be happy but sometimes I'm sad
I seem to be good but sometimes I'm bad
I seem to be childish but I'm an adult in disguise
I seem to be loud but really I'm kind
I seem to be blonde but most of it's fake
People judge me as a dizzy dumb blonde
But I'm not I'm a blonde in my own unique way.

Danika McDonagh (12)
St Mary & St Joseph's School, Sidcup

THE PHOTOGRAPHER

I saw him again yesterday.
There was a flash of light and a bang.
A mine in a nearby field.

Then he turned up . . .

With a click and a flash he tries to capture
The moment
But the moment is lost. Found only in the
Haunting memories of those who witnessed.

He moves on . . .

He sees a crowd. Huddled in a circle.
He rushes towards them. His camera in one hand
His morals in the other.
He grasps the camera with both hands and drops
His morals to the ground.

The crowd watches a woman dying at their feet.
He takes a picture.
Then another
Then another
Where are his morals?

They are behind him now!

David Beattie (16)
St Mary & St Joseph's School, Sidcup

LADY IN RED

I was looking in the mirror,
finishing my tie,
when I saw a faint character
in the corner of my eye.

She, an elderly lady, dressed in red,
she was walking towards me
scratching her head,

I completed my grooming by
combing my hair
and turned around sharpish
but nothing was there.

I looked back in the mirror as
she began to climb,
the stairs going up to room
three hundred and nine.

I thought this was strange as
I had been told,
room 309 was going to be sold.

The previous owner had died in
her bed,
dressed in her favourite colour . . .
red.

Charlie Sivell (12)
St Mary & St Joseph's School, Sidcup

THE FLOWER

A precious layer protecting a secret splendour,
Open. The beauty revealed.
Glory, a dance to a tender melody sweet to the ear.
Among thorns stands bold yet delicate and innocent to the world.
The passionate fragrance holds you in a daze of emotions,
kind to the soul, at peace with the heart.
Sadness. The beauty seems to slowly fade until one day,
the thorns seem sharper and bitter without the splendour
that was amongst its weaving bush,
Now seems plain.
To look back seems nothing,
the excitement has passed
now little more than a memory of this beauty shall last.

Clare Black (15)
St Mary & St Joseph's School, Sidcup

MOST PEOPLE THINK BUT . . .

Most people think I am getting taller
but I just think others are shrinking.
Most people think my appetite is growing
but I just think they are feeding me less.
Most people think I can swim further
but I just think the pool is shrinking.
Most people think I am quiet
but to me I'm just me.
I wish I knew what was going to happen
but then life might not be so fun.
I wish I knew when I was going to die
but the last moments might not be so special.

Scott Fry (13)
St Mary & St Joseph's School, Sidcup

FEAR THE FEMALE FLAME

I spot you in the dark,
Bright above the rest.
A warm, attractive light,
Unlike the others.
You don't hurt my eyes,
I am not put off or turned away,
Dramatically dancing in the darkness
Attractive at night.

I come closer
And you dance some more.
I feel your radiant heat,
I smile,
I am happy.
Little flame, you heat my heart and warm my soul.
So beautiful and warm.

I reach to touch you,
Your heat increases.
You throw a fast and frantic fit,
An electrifying dance.
Little flame, you mesmerise me.
I am excited and I tremble.
I feel you at my fingertips.

You stand so still,
You look so different.
Bright and unattractive.
My feelings fade
Like your light.
I am left alone in the dark,
Nursing the pain you leave me with.

Paul Husbands (16)
St Mary & St Joseph's School, Sidcup

FOOTBALL

It's Saturday, it's 3 o'clock
The players come out to kick-off
The whistle goes, the crowd all cheer
Some fans had not even got their beer
It's passed out wide, he crosses it in
A glancing header, oh it's in
2 minutes gone, it's 1-0
Oh my God, it's already 1-0!
They are on the attack, round the keeper
It's a penalty you stupid keeper!
He places the ball on the spot
The ball has stuck to the spot
He runs up to take it, he has slipped
He kicks the ball and he has missed
He has missed, what has he done?
He could have made the score 1-1
The whistle goes, it's time to go
The crowd leave the stadium really slow
1-0 the score, United win
I hope they win next week again.

David Gerrard (12)
St Mary & St Joseph's School, Sidcup

A BLOODY WAR

A girl sits in the corner,
Of a muddy field.
Bodies drop down to the ground
And turns brown puddles red.

It rains harder and gets colder,
She looks at the field.
Covered in red,
Blood-red.

A gunshot stops her train of thought,
A loud piercing gunshot.
Another body drops to the ground,
She shudders at the sound.

Does the murderer even care?
The families he's ripped apart.
For him a life long punishment,
Guilt?

Sarah Collins (12)
St Mary & St Joseph's School, Sidcup

TRAPPED

Any serenity that I feel disappears,
Just as the sunshine disappears into the night sky.
I feel trapped,
Like in a cold, dark cave with no way out.
Why do I feel this way?
Why does no one understand the unease that's here?
Why are there so many unanswerable questions
Floating around?
Why can't I have just one day -
To be free like a bird,
Soaring through a cloudless sky,
With no worries,
Just the feeling of freedom?
Yet reality would always return.
Life can be harsh and its harshness can hit you.
A rock can hit you,
Yet a rock can maybe, one day,
Sort everything out,
But only maybe.

Rebecca Pett (15)
St Mary & St Joseph's School, Sidcup

SOME DAY, ONE DAY

Some day, one day you'll have
that first day at school.
Some day, one day you'll have
that all important kiss
behind the bike sheds.
Some day, one day you'll get
your first promotion.
Some day, one day you'll find
a partner and get married.
Some day, one day you'll have
children a lovely home.
Some day, one day you'll be
king of the world.
Some day, one day you'll
experience the world end.
Some day, one day you'll die
and start a new life in a
different dimension.
This will happen to you
some day, one day in your
lifetime!

Katie Faurie (12)
St Mary & St Joseph's School, Sidcup

ME AND MY CRAZY FAMILY

My mum's a cracker, off her trolley,
My dad's a jerk, a bit of a wally.
My brother . . . well . . . where do I start?
We call him plastic man because of his hair,
Dare I touch it . . . phew . . . I wouldn't dare.
On goes the gel at the start of the day,
Will his hair move . . . phew . . . no way.

My nanny Pat's a cracker, that's for sure,
When she passes wind her feet come off the floor!
When she reads this poem, my eye she's gonna sock it,
For suggesting that her backside is just like a rocket!
Four generations going back to great nan,
Now you can see why I'm the loony
I am!

Sarah Cumings (11)
St Mary & St Joseph's School, Sidcup

MY NAN

My nan,
Why are nans as sweet as sweet,
So kind and thoughtful
And never cheat?

My nan is like an angel sent from heaven,
Father Christmas is no competition,
She sits on her chair,
Always correct and fair.

My nan is like a rocket scientist,
Always right and the wisest.

My nan is fantastic,
In every way,
So cheery and happy
And will always play.

Nan I love you in every way,
I love my nan more than words can say,
I never want my nan to go away.

James Tristram Smith (13)
St Mary & St Joseph's School, Sidcup

MY CAT'S FUNERAL

Bury her deep, down deep,
Safe in the earth's cold keep,
Bury her deep.

No more to watch birds stir,
No more to clean dark fur,
No more to glisten as silk,
No more to revel in milk,
No more to purr.

Bury her deep, down deep,
She is beyond warm sleep,
She will not walk in the night,
She will not wake in the light,
Bury her deep.

Stephen Mullan (12)
St Mary & St Joseph's School, Sidcup

I WISH I KNEW . . .

I wish I knew why I get cross,
but it's my brother, he thinks he's boss.

I wish I knew how to fly,
but I will fall out of the sky.

I wish I knew where to go,
but I am wandering down low.

I wish I knew why I seem bad,
but really I'm just sad.

I wish I knew the time,
but really I hope this rhymes.

Gareth Pritchard (12)
St Mary & St Joseph's School, Sidcup

STARTING SECONDARY SCHOOL

'Go to bed'
My mum said
'You've got an early start'
I've gone to bed
I can't sleep
I can hear the beating of my heart.

I'm at the bus stop
I can't turn back
This fear I have to face
It's like a square
Sixth form top
And I'm right at the base.

I'm at the school
I'm really nervous
The bell's about to go
Now I wish I hadn't come
I'm feeling really low.

I'm in my class
It's really good
My form teacher's really nice
The good thing is
He said he'd help us
And give us his advice.

It's home time now
Time to go
Now I'm feeling really low
I've had a good time
And I can't wait
To come back here tomorrow!

Anna Woodcock (11)
St Mary & St Joseph's School, Sidcup

PEOPLE SAY

People say that the world
spins round, but to me my feet
are still on the ground.

People say that the clouds hold water
but to me they are puffs of spongy cotton.

People say that the snow is cold, but to
me it's soft and rather mild.

People say that the sun is hot, but to me
it's a big glowing, shiny dot.

People say that the wind blows hard
but to me it's breezy and cool.
Sometimes I wonder if these things
are true, but then again, I say to
myself, it's always up
to you.

Elina Theodoulou (12)
St Mary & St Joseph's School, Sidcup

RATS

Rats are not scary,
They're just skinny and hairy,
With four feet each,
You'd be amazed how far they reach.

With red eyes at night,
They could give you a fright,
But when they are mine,
Well that's just fine.

Their colours just right,
A nice beige and white,
With whiskers shiny and long,
If you keep them clean
They won't pong.

With their ears so small,
To them we are so tall,
When they are so neat,
They always deserve a treat.

Sean Funnell (13)
St Mary & St Joseph's School, Sidcup

NINE PLANETS

Nine planets,
People know there's nine planets.
But I always wonder why
The stars and the galaxies
That haven't been seen fly by.
People know we have a sun,
But to me it's another star.
Planet X and other stars,
Just wonder off so far.
The beaming sun is not so good,
Any other star could have stood.
Nearest to the Earth burning away,
But the sun will have to stay.
Aliens are not real I tell myself,
We have love, we have health.
So people know there's nine planets,
But I will always wonder why.

William Lovell (12)
St Mary & St Joseph's School, Sidcup

STARTING SCHOOL

It was the first day of school
And I was nervous
As well as this I was excited too.
I packed my bags but was very
Cautious.
I didn't know what I would have to do.

At 8:10 there was a car outside
My mum walked me out to the cab
I arrived at school after a short ride
And I thought it was really fab

We went to Assembly then to our class
And wrote lots of things in our journals
After it felt like years, it was lunch at last
And soon our tummies were full.

Gregory Walker (11)
St Mary & St Joseph's School, Sidcup

WHAT IS LOVE?

What is love?
Love is loving your mum and dad
To love your girlfriend or to love the world itself
Love is the strongest thing in the world
Bigger than money
What is love?
Love is scoring the winning goal
Or crossing the winning line
What is love?
Love is the giving and receiving of presents
And the pleasure it brings.

Daniel Dill (12)
St Mary & St Joseph's School, Sidcup

THE TEST

Tick-tock, tick-tock,
Goes the awful climbing clock.
The question's turning, swirling, turning,
My head is burning, flaming, burning.
The pencil's scratching, tearing away,
Stop, stop, stop I say.
The footsteps walking through my brain,
Oh don't tell me I might be insane.
Then all like a gunshot,
Or a highwayman's plot,
The clock suddenly stopped.
I froze, the ice walked up my legs,
The end, it's over, bell rings.

Emma Duggan (13)
St Mary & St Joseph's School, Sidcup

THE WORLD

The world is
round as round as
can be that is how it is
to me

It spins and spins all
day long and that is how it
belongs

Pollution can damage
the earth and the
whole universe.

Hollie Langley (12)
St Mary & St Joseph's School, Sidcup

RIOT

The riot is smelt in the air,
Violence is seen everywhere,
There are bodies in my way,
Shouldn't have come out to play,
The eyes are sore and there's stinging in the face,
The painful effects of Mace,
As I drown in the crowd,
The gunshots seem so loud,
Like a volcano that's been dormant
For a hundred years,
The crowd burst out in rage and angry tears,
My nose starts to flatten
And they still hit it with a baton,
The cold blood drips down my neck,
I notice that the streets are in a wreck,
The thumpers thumping
And the blood is rushing,
The head is spinning
And the eyes are raining,
Destruction, chaos, blood and gore,
A lazy politician caused this war.

Anucha Forbes (15)
St Mary & St Joseph's School, Sidcup

I WONDER IN THE NIGHT

I wonder in the night if there are monsters
hiding underneath my bed.

I wonder in the night if there are witches
in my cupboard, stirring a poison.

I wonder in the night if there are devils
hanging from the ceiling.

I get out of my bed, step down on to the ground,
I think to myself, the monster is going to grab
my foot and pull me under the bed.

But as I stand there waiting and shivering in fear . . .

Nothing happens!

Kesha Toussaint (12)
St Mary & St Joseph's School, Sidcup

MY HORRIBLE FIRST DAY

I got up and got dressed
My uniform was nice
My mum told me not to worry
But I was under stress.

I was scared of the older kids
What if they want to fight?
I wanted to go home
Or get the day over and done with.

I got into class . . .
My tummy turned, what if I get picked on
I sat down all alone, the teacher said
'Why are you sitting alone looking shy
Come and make some friends
You're not going to die.'

But now I'm OK
I've got some friends which are kind
The teachers are fine
And the older kids . . . well they're OK too!

Fern Fitzgerald (11)
St Mary & St Joseph's School, Sidcup

HERBIE MY FRIEND

H appy is his wagging tail
E ars in a water bowl, sloppy and wet
R unning fast chasing his ball
B ig brown eyes, sad but alert
I ntelligent and smart, doesn't miss a trick
E njoys a fuss and a friend to play with.

M uscles solid and he knocks you over
Y ou'll never find a better friend.

F ootprints of mud on the kitchen floor
R abbits, pheasants and pigeons he chases
I nto everything, my trainers he pinches
E nergetic, he's always on the go
N utty and crazy a real loony dog
D evoted, I know I'm his friend too.

Paul Cumings (13)
St Mary & St Joseph's School, Sidcup

GHOST

There was a ghost that used to frighten me,
He came to me at night
And gave me such a fright,
Because that was the last thing I expected see
A ghost so near to me.

At first he would catch me unaware,
The way he would sit and stare,
But then I got used to him being there.

He told me all about his life,
He used to live in this house with his wife
And how she died of a sudden death,
That's the reason he never left.

I told him to go and look for her,
That would be the only way to find her if he loves her
So . . .

Danielle McGoldrick (13)
St Mary & St Joseph's School, Sidcup

Dogs!

Dogs are large
and can be small.
The smaller the cuter,
the bigger the badder.

Black, white,
brown or golden.
All the colours you can get.

Mean dogs, sweet dogs,
rough dogs, tough dogs,
bad dogs, mad dogs,
anyone you choose to buy.

Teach the dog a lot of tricks
and give it a lot of treats.
Loveable, dislikable,
but always there for you.

Zoe Fernandes (13)
St Mary & St Joseph's School, Sidcup

My Mum...

My mum is no way dumb,
in fact she's cool, wicked and fun,
but sometimes I get a fright,
because somehow she's always right.
I love my mum no matter what,
even if she's a fussy pot.
She can be nice,
she can be mean,
on top of that she's a working machine.
There are some days where she will rest
and I clean the house my very best,
but that's not often 'obviously'.
It's always Mum doing things for me
and she always says 'Do well at school
and please don't break another rule.'
And when I do she's really mad,
but now I'm gonna make her glad.
Oh I don't know what I would do,
or what life would be without my mum
next to me!

Dee Robinson (13)
St Mary & St Joseph's School, Sidcup

I Wonder If?

I wonder if there are aliens patrolling the midnight sky.
I wonder if they think about us thinking 'I wonder if and why?'
I wonder if they say 'May be some aliens are out there.'
I wonder if they wonder like us saying 'But where?'
'I wonder if' is all both worlds can say.
I wonder if like us they think about us every day.

Siobhan O'Neill (12)
St Mary & St Joseph's School, Sidcup

USELESS

You're as useless
as a bullet without a gun
as the sky without the sun
as a wall without a brick
as a clock without a tick

As useless
as a dog without its woof
as a house without its roof
as a dog without its bark
as the night without the dark

As useless
as a car without its engine
and the Antarctic without a penguin
as a clock without its hand
and the beach without the sand
as the sun without its rays
as a week without its days

As useless
as a sheep without its wool
as a pupils without their school
as a bear without its hair
as a lion without its lair

You're as useless
as a garden full of weeds
and a cheetah without its speed
as a fire without its flame
and an archer without his aim.

Nicholas Thomas (12)
St Mary & St Joseph's School, Sidcup

MILLENNIUM

At the end of the year we celebrate
A unique and a once in a lifetime date
At parties champagne corks will pop
As people count down on the clock.

Why do the happy people cheer?
Is it because it's a new year?
For all the time has now come
To celebrate a new millennium.

What will happen in the next thousand years?
Will it be happy or will it be tears?
Will computers rule the world over?
Will robots let us live in clover?

May be we will travel to Mars
May be we'll go beyond the stars
One thing for sure, that I know
I will not be here for the next show.

Michael McGlone (11)
St Mary & St Joseph's School, Sidcup

I SEEM TO BE BUT . . .

I seem to be loud but I am very shy,
I seem to be arrogant but I just like to do things well,
I seem to be neat but I only take pride in my work,
I seem to be talkative but I only hide my fears,
I seem to be boring but I am really bubbly,
I seem to be different but to my family I am special.

Ingrid Elad (12)
St Mary & St Joseph's School, Sidcup

I Seem To Be . . .

I am a 13 year old girl in a big, big world
I try to act big, but really I am small.

I am quite confident but that's just how it looks
I really am shy but that you can't see.

I am quite friendly but I do have nasty ways
You can trust me with your secrets,
I'll never let you down.

I am proud of the way I am
But I wish for things, I know I have to wait to have.

Leigh-Anne Morrison (13)
St Mary & St Joseph's School, Sidcup

Giraffes

See that giraffe over there
Look at its yellow and brown hair
Look at its neck, so skinny and tall
Compared with us, we're so small.

It eats leaves on trees,
Gets stung by bees,
Look at its feet,
So small and neat.

Its teeth are so yellow,
For such a big fellow,
Its tongue is so thick
With a big soggy lick.

Luke Oxlade (13)
St Mary & St Joseph's School, Sidcup

My Mates

My mates are a bundle of fun
and when we meet up the laughs have just begun.
We're trendy, we're cool, we're daring too,
we love a good time and we'll show you.

We're perky, we're cheeky and all get along
and when we party we have a sing song.
We love to eat and eat all day,
we eat burgers, chips and milkshakes away.

We love to shop and shop till we drop
and once we start we never want to stop.
We'll buy and buy till we can't buy any more,
we'll go in every shop and even every store.

Those are my mates and they are all summed up
hope you like my poem as my time is up.

Zoe Purpuri (13)
St Mary & St Joseph's School, Sidcup

Unknown

The unknown is everywhere.
Day and night it's everywhere.
In ghosts, in devils it's there.
Does this unknown exist?
Are there ghosts in the unknown?
Who knows?
It's the unknown!

Jemma Gillis (13)
St Mary & St Joseph's School, Sidcup

TELEVISION - A LOVE HATE RELATIONSHIP

I turn on the tele
Some freak has been watching 5

I pick up the channel zapper
I turn it to 4, OK
3, lower
2, almost time
1, I'm mellowing in my own self pity.

The only thing worth the cash is the VCR
On it I can watch
The adventures of
Steed, Templar, Bond.

Roger Moore and Ian Ogilvy as Templar
Connery, Lazenby, Moore, Dalton and Brosnan as Bond
All can be watched in peace
No advertisements, sponsors or anything else
Bliss.

I can also stop and start when I like
No panicking over what I'm going to miss.

God bless the man who created it
Love that man!

Simon Northwood (12)
St Mary & St Joseph's School, Sidcup

SOPPY LOVE

Love is soppy
Love is stupid
There is no point
Of little old Cupid

My brother thinks
It's great
He has a girlfriend
He is only eight

Help my brother
God help my brother
He's so stupid
He believes in love
Yuck, gooey
Soppy love
Get rid of it
Before I grow up.

Kirsty Lake (11)
St Mary & St Joseph's School, Sidcup

LOVE

There they stood in the dim moonlight
Holding hands and walking along the smooth, sandy beach.
The sea stayed calm while the trees swayed softly.
They stood there like trees rooted to the ground.
They looked into each other's eyes,
Like a deer looks into water.

Nicky Singh (11)
St Mary & St Joseph's School, Sidcup

THE CONFUSION OF BEING A TEENAGER

What a day I've had, not a thing went right
When I got up today, someone had broken the light
I got into school, I was half an hour late
Someone's spreading rumours, I bet it's my best mate

When I get home I'll make some food
Has mum been shopping, there was nothing good
Fifty-three biscuits and a pint of Coke
Do you think one more biscuit would make me choke?

I can't got my homework, I've lost my favourite pen
What's this on my telly about ladies that are men
Tomorrow I've got maths I bet she's in a mood
She's always out to get me, I suppose I should be good

Last night, I watched my team play, 7-0 the final score
Goal, their leagues so easy, it's getting quite a bore
Today I dumped my girlfriend, she was getting up my nose
One day she took her shoes off, she had hairy toes

The lads are off to Millwall, to see the rubbish blues
I'm not quite that sad yet, I'm off to buy new shoes
I'll wear my shoes tonight, I'm going on the pull
You want to hear from me for a while, my diary is completely full

My dinner is on the plate, I'll have to say goodbye
Oh what is smelling? I hope it's chicken pie
Oh yeah! Mum, dentists tomorrow at ten
Oi! Come back is that my favourite pen.

Chris Carmichael (15)
St Mary & St Joseph's School, Sidcup

JERRY SPRINGER

As the camera rolls the crowd goes wild,
With a hundred cheers of 'Jerry'.
Feet are jumping, hands are clapping,
With a hundred cheers of 'Jerry'.
Bodyguards are shattered, women are battered.
To a hundred cheers of 'Jerry'.
Feet are flying, women are crying
To a hundred cheers of 'Jerry'.
People are laughing, men are starting,
To a hundred cheers of 'Jerry'.
Jerry stands up, 'I've had enough!'
To a hundred cheers of 'Jerry'.

Thomas Ford (11)
St Mary & St Joseph's School, Sidcup

LUNCH

I can't wait for lunch - munch, munch, munch
Crisps and chocolate - crunch, crunch, crunch
Oh what a big bunch going for lunch
Rushing to the hall and queuing for us all
Rumbling tummies we can hear it all
Oh to find a seat to eat it all
Our tummies are full, let's rush from the hall
Out into the playground, to talk and play and have some fun
There the bell goes, we finish our fun
Back to our work for everyone.

Laura Finn (11)
St Mary & St Joseph's School, Sidcup

FRIENDS

Friends should never turn away
Friends should face my way
Friends should never say go away
Friends should always say come my way

Friends should never fight with friends
They should be there till the end
Friends should always love their friends
Friends never steal their boyfriends

Friends should go shopping
Friends should turn up on time
And don't leave with a person they don't like
Tom Bell!

Carla Cunningham (13)
St Mary & St Joseph's School, Sidcup

MY BABY SISTER

I have a baby sister,
I love her every day,
Her name is Sarah,
Hip, hip, hooray.

I can't wait till she gets older
And she can run around
And when I hold her,
She tries to reach the ground.

I can't wait till she talks,
So I hear her speak,
Soon she'll drink water,
And it's a pity she'll leak!

Philip Crompton (13)
The King Ethelbert School

SOMETHING I HATE... HOMEWORK

Something I hate, we get at least once a day.
It used to take up all my time,
So I'd just throw it away.
I'd rip it, I'd tear it, if I could,
But when in school, it wouldn't look very good.
Now I'm wiser and older,
I do it and put it in a folder.
Division, dividing,
Oh it's so much writing.
Writing's so boring,
Why can't it be drawing?
The plague, the Black Death,
We're reading Macbeth.
When my homework is the best,
It gets put up above the rest.
So I guess I can't be the one to groan,
Because if I don't do it,
It will be moan, moan, moan.
At least it isn't all my time,
If it was, it would be whine, whine, whine.

Michael Hilton (14)
The King Ethelbert School

MY IDEAL CAR

My ideal car would be sporty and fast,
My ideal car would take off with a blast,
My ideal car would be yellow and blue,
My ideal car would be a Z3 BMW.

My ideal car would have a big exhaust pipe,
My ideal car would be a particular type,
My ideal car would have a tan interior,
My ideal car would make a Ferrari look inferior.

Simon Smith-Robbie (13)
The King Ethelbert School

QUEUING

Queuing is dull, boring.
What is the point of standing around like a tree?
What is the point of wasting time like a hippo?
What is the point of getting aches like a bug?
Queuing is for people who have nothing to do.
Queuing, standing, slouching, it all bugs me.
Queuing next to people who sweat like a waterfall,
Queuing next to people who have bad breath like a dog,
Queuing next to people who stare like a meerkat,
People who look at what ever you're doing,
Like you're a clown.
People asking annoying questions,
people who do not move forward when there is space,
Like they are a brick.
People who talk to the cashier about babies, pets, holidays,
Like they know them.
People who have nothing else to do.
Queuing is boring,
But other people do,
But most annoying of all is when someone in front of a queue
Is in front of you!

Darren Oxborrow (14)
The King Ethelbert School

CATS

I hate cats!
They always miaow,
and are mostly fat.
They hiss and bite,
and scratch and fight!

I hate cats!
They come in different shapes and sizes,
thin, fat, big and little.
They come in different colours and shapes,
white, creamy, black and brown.

I hate cats!
They climb trees and get stuck,
to get down they'll need a truck.
One good thing, they catch a mouse
that is lying around your house.

But still . . . I hate cats!

Natalie Baker (13)
The King Ethelbert School

RATS

I wanted a pet bat,
My mum said 'Have a rat.'
I already had a cat,
On which I'd never sat.

I thought I'd call it Eddie,
But when the time was ready,
I decided to get two,
They make a lot of poo.

So Rodent is the other,
He is tougher than his brother.
He always takes the nice food,
When he is in a bad mood.

I hope when they get older,
They'll still sit on my shoulder.
When people see their tails,
They scream - it never fails!

Lee Joiner (11)
The King Ethelbert School

FIRST DAY AT SCHOOL

The school is much bigger than I thought,
But now I am used to it,
It's not that bad.

I thought that carrying all my books to
Different classrooms would be difficult,
But it's not that bad.

I thought that everyone would laugh at me,
But they don't.
It's not that bad.

I thought it would be impossible
To make new friends, but
it's not that bad.

At my old school we didn't have
Big machines and saws to worry me, but
It's not that bad.

Daniel Farrier (11)
The King Ethelbert School

THE WITCH'S SPELL

Red flames that shoot up to the sky,
We witches hear you cry.
Frankenstein's stitches,
Ten dead witches,
Snow White's poisoned apple,
We witches cackle.

A clap of thunder,
We go down under,
A black cat's tale,
A big, friendly whale,
A chicken's beak,
Do not peek.

This is when the spell ends,
It's sure to send you round the bend.

Joanne Lamb (12)
The King Ethelbert School

SOMETHING I HATE

Something I hate is smaller than me,
It lurks in its bedroom upstairs.
It annoys me everywhere I go,
It loves Tinky Winky, Laa Laa, Dipsy and Po.
It has got the ugliest face,
I wish it would just leave this place.
It has a mouth like the rear of a horse,
Who is it? My brother, of course.

Steven Lloyd (13)
The King Ethelbert School

DEATH

I hate death,
Don't you?
Hospitals, drips and things like that,
First my cousin, then my nan,
Who's going to be next?
I hate death, don't you?

I hate death,
Old people die, young people die
And babies die.
Death is unfair.
I hate death, don't you?
You can die of lots of things,
Diseases, old age, still-birth, road accidents,
I hate death, don't you?
Sometimes it's a long death,
Sometimes it's a quick death,
Death is unfair.
I hate death, don't you?

I hate death,
Funerals, flowers and things like that,
First my cousin, then my nan,
Who's going to be next?
I hate death, don't you?

I hate death,
Graves, crosses and things like that.
First my cousin, then my nan,
Who's going to be next?
I hate death, don't you?

Claire Lewis (13)
The King Ethelbert School

Shopping

I hate going shopping,
In supermarkets mostly.
The total boringness,
Of walking aimlessly.

The whole concept,
Of walking around with a trolley,
Choosing things here and there,
Brussels, carrots and broccoli.

Boring stuff,
In a boring place,
Try and get it over and done with,
But something catches your eye, so you slow your pace.

And when you get used to it,
After a while,
You get to know where things are,
And what they do?
Change around the aisles!

Oh, how I hate going shopping!
But . . .! I like going with my mum,
Because she always buys me sweets and chocolate,
Now that's what I call an upside
Yum! Yum!

Lauren Pointer (13)
King Ethelbert School

SOMETHING I HATE . . .

The things I hate are spiders,
And the way the wretched things look,
They sit on the wall and stare at you
As if to say, 'Don't you dare throw that book!'
But what they don't know yet,
Is that I'll soon get my own back,
By squashing them with my shoe.
The things I hate are spiders
And their long, hairy legs,
They run across your bedroom wall,
Then *bang,* the horrid thing is dead!

Joanne Gough (13)
The King Ethelbert School

SOMETHING I HATE

When rain starts pouring,
Life seems really boring.
I hate being kept inside,
When I could be on a theme park ride.
We play board games around the fire,
I am starting to get very tired,
The day is coming to an end,
My little brother's going round the bend.
I've started to fall asleep,
I've gone, really, really deep.
I'll wake up to find the rain has gone,
But in its place there shines the sun!

Leeroy Fairhurst (13)
The King Ethelbert School

Something I Hate

Something I hate you have to do most nights,
It's so boring, it makes golf look good,
It goes on and on and never stops,
It's given to you in large amounts,
Enough to make you go mad.
Teachers even love you not being able to do it,
'Oh you should have listened,' they said,
'Then you would know what to do.'
Some of it requires research
To find out about your task,
Sometimes you need to ask questions,
Questions so hard, they can't be answered,
Even when you have completed it
To the very best of your standards,
There is always somebody who is better.
But once a year, my homework is the best
And gets put up on display.

James Lee (13)
The King Ethelbert School

Something I Hate

Something I hate
Is surrounding us,
It's always there,
It causes a fuss.

I hate it, it's stupid,
It annoys me so much,
They're pathetic and ignorant,
But they don't usually touch.

They've got all the mouth,
They give it the looks,
They're always there,
Peering above the books.

By now you should have guessed
What it is -
Ignorance,
Yes, of course it is.

Hannah Swinton (13)
The King Ethelbert School

MY PAPER ROUND

I hate getting up on a Monday morning.
The alarm goes off and the rain is pouring.

I get out of my bed and into something
That should hold out the wet.

I open the gate and off I go,
On my bike through the snow

But by the end of the week
All my money is spent,

Goes to the people who gave
Or lent.

I realise it's Saturday and I get paid,
The wages of £15 go straight away.

I owe it all to the people who lent

And that's another day and it's back
To the dreaded morning of Monday.

Shaun Jarman (13)
The King Ethelbert School

Something I Hate

They are grown in a muddy field,
they are the farmers' yield.
Then they sell them in a market,
right next to the parsnips.
Mothers buy them by the kilogram,
take them home and boil them in a pan.
They dish them on a plate,
an innocent child's plate,
then the child is forced to eat them,
but not me. I refuse them.
I'm told they're good for me,
I'm told to clean my plate,
but to be honest, I would rather eat a sour grape.
These things I hate are green,
These things I hate are small,
These things I hate are round,
These things I hate are sprouts.

Claire Westcott (13)
The King Ethelbert School

Something I Hate

Something I hate is creepy and crawly,
With a little round body and eight long legs.
They sit and wait
For flies, caught in their webs.

They drop down from trees
And crawl across your knees,
They tangle in your hair,
They seem to be everywhere.

People say I take after my mum,
But she hates wasps and bees that hum,
She also can't stand mice,
But I think they're rather nice.

But what I really hate,
What I really can't stand is . . .
Spiders!

Kelly Davenport (13)
The King Ethelbert School

FIRST DAY AT SECONDARY SCHOOL

Tall people bigger than me,
Carrying bags everywhere,
Playground, canteen,
You can have a choice of food.
Science labs different,
Many more teachers
Than at primary school.
I was afraid of telling people,
I stuttered.
It's so much bigger,
Lots more homework,
Different kinds of subjects
Every day.
Different teachers in each class,
So many more children
At secondary school.

Michael Helder (11)
The King Ethelbert School

THE FIRST DAY AT SECONDARY SCHOOL

Slowly coming through, through the gates -
People are looking at me,
My heart is pounding faster and faster -
People are looking at me,
Walking slowly into the hall, seeing my friends -
People are looking at me,
Going to our tutor groups -
People are looking at me,
Seeing new people -
People are looking at me,
Being with new and old friends -
People are looking at me,
And I am looking at people.

Emma Hamlington (11)
The King Ethelbert School

FIRST DAY AT SCHOOL

Lots of children all in blue,
Everyone saying, 'Who are you?'

Leather shoes and polished floor,
Squeaky shoes and slamming doors.

Nervous feeling all day long,
They're getting worse, the pips have gone.

I'm feeling happy to see my friends,
But frightened, where do all the
Damned corridors end!

Lauren Kidd (11)
The King Ethelbert School

FIRST DAY AT SCHOOL

I pull up to a great big school
And step out of the car.
People running everywhere,
What do I do now?
This place is so big and scary,
Will I fit in here?
I'll have to wait to find that out,
But I'll try my very best.
The day goes very quickly,
It doesn't seem so bad,
If things go well again tomorrow,
I will be very glad.
This big school thing is frightening,
But not so bad.

Simon Hale (11)
The King Ethelbert School

THE SEA

Oh I wish I could swim in the sea,
The crystal light shining down on me.
Different fishes, all kinds and sizes,
Go to the funfair, you'll win them as prizes.
Exotic and blue,
Dolphins are too.
The coral's multi-colours glistening in the sun,
Oh I wish I could swim in the sea,
I know it'll be fun.
The day has closed in now,
I'm waiting for another day to come,
So I can go back and swim in the sun.

Cassie Provan (12)
Thomas Aveling School

THE POEM FOR MANCHESTER UNITED

Man United, Man United, Man United,
The best, the best, the best.
They can beat the rest, rest, rest,
With Yorke, Giggs, Beckham, Cole,
They will always score super goals.
Man United, they're at the top,
They will surely never drop.
Man United won the treble, treble, treble,
With Sheringham, Solskjaer, Gary Neville.
They will never, never lose.
Who makes football great?
Man United, Man United, Man United,
The sport is fun and great, the best.
What is it?
Football, football, football.
Manchester United, simply the best,
The Red Devils.

Matthew Peskett (12)
Thomas Aveling School

BEST FRIENDS

We used to be best friends,
Which we are not anymore.
We used to be like needle and cotton,
But that's the way we were.
So why should we break up all over a silly thing?
So shall we be best friends, like we used to be?
But if you don't want to,
I will say farewell and goodbye.

Kerrie Lee (12)
Thomas Aveling School

TREES

Trees are enormous things that dominate the land,
They're big and they're small,
Birds nest in them,
Children climb them and
They're all over the land,
But people cut them, they saw them,
Then they try to sell them again.
This is a routine that is always seen,
But nothing is done about it.
With their enormous branches and green bushes
They are the world's lungs that breathe.
Our oxygen comes from them, that we need,
But if they're not there, we will never see them again.
Without our trees, the land would be bare
And nothing green would ever be seen.
So this is my message to all the world
Where all the tree-cutters are seen.
Stop cutting our trees!

Steve Mashiter (13)
Thomas Aveling School